The Life of Galileo

Galileo confirms Copernicus' theories by the use of a telescope but, afraid that a rational approach to science might spread to religion, the Inquisition puts Copernicus' teachings on the index. After eight years of silence, Galileo continues his research on his own theories, but the Inquisition's threat of torture frightens him into abjuring them. The Church allows him to write a treatise on Motion, but the manuscript is removed as he writes it. Galileo has, however, made two copies and the second is eventually smuggled out of Italy.

The play was written in 1938–39 and in 1945–47. An English version made by Brecht in collaboration with Charles Laughton was first produced at Beverly Hills, California, in 1947 with Laughton as Galileo. The present version is a translation of the complete text of the latest German edition, not a stage adaptation.

The Life of Galileo

BY

BERTOLT BRECHT

translated by Desmond I. Vesey

EYRE METHUEN

LONDON

All inquiries concerning the rights for
professional or amateur stage production should
be directed to the
International Copyright Bureau Ltd,
26 Charing Cross Road, London, WC2

*Paperback edition first published in Great Britain
in 1963
Reprinted 1964, 1965, 1966
Reprinted 1968 and 1971
Reprinted 1974 by Eyre Methuen
This translation copyright © 1960
by Desmond I. Vesey;
original work published under the title of*
LEBEN DES GALILEI
*copyright 1955 by Suhrkamp Verlag, Berlin
Printed in Great Britain
by Cox & Wyman Ltd
Fakenham, Norfolk*
SBN 413 32040 5

THE AUTHOR'S NOTES ON
'THE LIFE OF GALILEO'*

FOREWORD

IT is well known how felicitously people can be influenced by the conviction that they are poised on the threshold of a new age. At such a moment their environment appears to be still entirely unfinished, capable of the happiest improvements, full of dreamt of and undreamt of possibilities, like malleable raw material in their hands. They themselves feel as if they have awakened to a new day – rested, strong, resourceful. Old beliefs are dismissed as superstitions, what yesterday seemed a matter of course is today subject to fresh examination. We have been ruled, says mankind, but now we shall be the rulers.

Around the turn of this century no other line from a song so powerfully inspired the workers as the line: 'Now a new age is dawning'; old and young marched to it, the poorest, the down-and-outs and those who had already won something of civilisation for themselves – all felt young. Under a house-painter the unprecedented power of corruption of these self-same words was also tried and proved; for he, too, promised a new age. Here the words revealed their emptiness and imprecision. Their strength lay in their very indefiniteness, which was now being exploited in demoralising the masses. The new age – that was something and is something that affects everything, leaves nothing unchanged, but is, also, still only unfolding its character gradually; something in which all imagination has scope to flower, and which is only restricted by too precise description. Glorious is the feeling of beginning, of pioneering; the fact of being a beginner inspires enthusiasm. Glorious is the feeling of happiness in those who oil a new machine before it displays its strength,

* Brecht was not able to assemble and prepare these notes for publication. They are printed in their unedited form. (Elisabeth Hauptmann)

in those who fill in a blank space on an old map, in those who dig the foundation of a new house, their house.

This feeling comes to the researcher who makes a discovery that will change everything, to the orator who prepares a speech that will create an entirely new situation. Terrible is the disappointment when men discover, or think they discover, that they have fallen victims to an illusion, that the old is stronger than the new, that the 'facts' are against them and not for them, that their age – the new age – has not yet arrived. Then, things are not merely as bad as before, but much worse because people have made immense sacrifices for their schemes and have lost everything; they have ventured and are now defeated; the old is taking its revenge on them. The researcher or the discoverer – an unknown, but also unpersecuted man before he has published his discovery – when once his discovery has been disproved or discredited is a swindler and a charlatan, and all too well known; the victim of oppression and exploitation, when once his insurrection has been crushed, is a rebel who is subject to special repression and punishment. Exertion is followed by exhaustion, possibly exaggerated hope by possibly exaggerated hopelessness. Those who do not relapse into indifference and apathy fall into worse; those who have not sacrificed their energies for their ideals, now turn those selfsame energies against those very ideals! There is no more remorseless reactionary than a frustrated innovator, no crueller enemy of the wild elephant than the tame elephant.

And yet these disappointed men may still go on existing in a new age, an age of great upheaval. Only, they know nothing of new ages.

In these days the conception of the 'New' is itself falsified. The Old and the Very Old, now re-entering the arena, proclaim themselves as New; or else it is held to be new when the Old or the Very Old are put over in a new way. But the really New, having been deposed today, is declared old-fashioned, degraded to being a transitory phase whose day is done. The 'new', for example, is the system of waging wars; whereas the 'old', so they say, is a system of economy, proposed but never put into practice, which would make wars superfluous. In the new system, society is being entrenched in classes; and the old, so they say, is the desire to abolish classes. The hopes of mankind do not so much become discouraged in these times; rather, they become diverted. Men had hoped that one day there would be bread to eat. Now they may hope that one day there will be stones to eat.

Amid the darkness gathering fast over a fevered world, a world enveloped by bloody deeds and no less bloody thoughts, by increasing barbarism which seems to be leading irresistibly to perhaps the greatest and most terrible war of all time, it is difficult to adopt an attitude appropriate to people on the threshold of a new and happier age. Does not everything point to night's arrival and nothing to the dawning of a new age? So shouldn't one, therefore, assume an attitude appropriate to people heading towards night?

What is this talk of a 'New Age'? Is not this expression itself obsolete? When it is shouted at us, it is bellowed from hoarse throats. Now, indeed, it is mere barbarism which impersonates the new age. It says of itself that it hopes it will last a thousand years.

So should one hold fast to the old times? Should one discuss sunk Atlantis?

Am I already lying down for the night and thinking, when I think of the morning, of the morning that has passed, so as to avoid thinking of the one to come? Is that why I pre-occupy myself with that era when the arts and sciences flowered three hundred years ago? I hope not.

These images of the morning and the night are misleading. Happy times do not come in the same way as a morning follows a night's sleep.

UNVARNISHED PICTURE OF A NEW AGE

Preamble to an American Version

When, during my first years in exile in Denmark, I wrote the play *The Life of Galileo*, I was helped in the reconstruction of the Ptolemaic cosmology by assistants of Niels Bohr who were working on the problem of 'splitting' the atom. My intention was, among others, to give an unvarnished picture of a new age – a strenuous undertaking since all those around me were convinced that our own era lacked every attribute of a new age. Nothing of this aspect had changed when, years later, I began, together with Charles Laughton, to prepare an American version of the play. The 'atomic' age made its debut at Hiroshima in the middle of our work. Overnight the biography of the founder of the new system of physics read differently. The infernal effect of the Great Bomb placed the conflict between Galileo and the authorities of his day in a new, a sharper light. We had to make only a few alterations – not a single one to the structure of the play. Already in the original version the Church was portrayed as a secular authority, its ideology as, fundamentally, interchangeable with many others. From the first, the key-stone of the gigantic figure of Galileo was his conception of science for the people. For hundreds of years and throughout the whole of Europe, people had paid him the honour, in the Galileo legend, of not believing in his recantation, just as they had for long derided scientists as biased, unpractical and eunuch-like old fogeys. (Even the term 'scholar' has something ridiculous about it; it has something 'downtrodden', something passive to it. In Bavaria people used to speak of the 'Nuremberg Funnel' through which, more or less forcibly, vast quantities of knowledge could be poured into mentally feeble persons – a sort of brain-enema. They were none the wiser for it. Also, if a person made a great show of cleverness, this was regarded as unnatural behaviour. The 'educated' – and to this word, too, there attaches that fatal flavour of passivity – spoke of the revenge of the 'uneducated', of an inborn hatred for the 'intellect', and, in fact, their contempt had frequently an admixture of hate; in the villages and in the suburbs the 'intellect' was felt to be alien and even hostile. But even among the 'better classes' this contempt was to be found. There was the 'scholarly world', and it was a different world. The 'scholar' was an impotent, bloodless, eccentric figure, 'stuck up' and not very capable of coping with life.)

Postscript to the American Production*

It must be understood that our production took place at the time, and in the country, of the production of the atom bomb and of its use for military purposes: when atomic physics was wrapped in impenetrable secrecy. The day the bomb was dropped will be difficult to forget for anyone who experienced it in the United States. It was the Japanese war which had cost America her real sacrifices. The troop transports went off from the West Coast, and returned there with the wounded and the victims of Asiatic diseases. When the first news reports reached Los Angeles, people knew that this meant the end of the detested war, the return of sons and brothers. But the great city gave an astonishing display of grief. The present writer heard bus-conductors and sales-girls in the fruit markets express nothing but horror. This was victory; but there was a bitter savour of defeat about it. Then came the secretiveness of the politicians and the military about this gigantic source of energy – secrecy which infuriated the in-tellectuals. The freedom of research, the exchange of information about discoveries, the international fellowship of scientists were clamped down on by officials who were deeply mistrusted. Great physicists fled precipitately from the service of their militaristic government; one of the most celebrated took a teaching job which compelled him to waste his working time at teaching the most elementary fundamentals of physics, in order not to have to serve under these officials. It had become a disgrace to discover anything.

PRAISE OR CONDEMNATION OF GALILEO?

It would be a great weakness in this work if those physicists were right who said to me – in a tone of approval – that Galileo's recantation of his teachings was, despite one or two 'waverings', portrayed as being sensible, with the argument that this recanta-tion enabled him to carry on with his scientific work and to hand it down to posterity. The fact is that Galileo enriched astronomy and physics by simultaneously robbing these sciences of a greater

* Summer, 1947, at Beverly Hills, California, with Charles Laughton as Galileo.

part of their social importance. By discrediting the Bible and the
Church, these sciences stood for a while at the barricades on
behalf of all progress. It is true that a swing-back took place in
the following centuries, and these sciences were involved in it,
but it was in fact a swing instead of a revolution; the scandal, so
to speak, degenerated into a dispute between experts. The Church,
and with it all the forces of reaction, was able to bring off an
organised retreat and more or less reassert its power. As far as
these particular sciences are concerned, they never again regained
their high position in society, neither did they ever again come
into such close contact with the people.

Galileo's crime can be regarded as the 'original sin' of modern
natural sciences. From the new astronomy, which deeply interested a new class – the bourgeoisie – since it gave an impetus to
the revolutionary social current of the time, he made a sharply
defined special science which – admittedly through its very 'pur-
ity', i.e. its indifference to modes of production – was able to
develop comparatively undisturbed. The atom bomb is, both as
a technical and as a social phenomenon, the classical end-product
of his contribution to science and his failure to society.

Thus, the 'hero' of this work is not Galileo but the people, as
Walter Benjamin has said. This seems to me to be rather too
briefly expressed. I hope this work shows what society extorts
from its individuals, what it needs from them. The urge to research, a social phenomenon no less delightful or compulsive
than the urge to reproduce, steers Galileo into that most dangerous territory, drives him into agonising conflict with his violent
desires for other pleasures. He raises his telescope to the stars
and delivers himself to the rack. In the end he indulges his science
like a vice, secretly and probably with pangs of conscience. Con-
fronted with such a situation, one can scarcely wish only to praise
or only to condemn Galileo.

'THE LIFE OF GALILEO' IS NOT A TRAGEDY

So, from the point of view of the theatre, the question will
arise whether *The Life of Galileo* is to be presented as a tragedy
or as an optimistic play. Is the keynote to be found in Galileo's

'Salutation to the New Age' in Scene 1 or in certain parts of
Scene 13? According to the prevalent rules of play-construction,
the end of a drama must carry the greater weight. But this play
is not constructed according to these rules. The play shows the
dawn of a new age and tries to correct some of the prejudices
about the dawn of a new age.

PORTRAYAL OF THE CHURCH

For the theatre it is important to understand that this play
must lose a great part of its effect if its performance is directed
chiefly against the Catholic Church. Of the dramatis personae,
many wear the Church's garb. Actors who, because of that, try
to portray these characters as odious would be doing wrong. Yet
neither, on the other hand, has the Church the right to have the
human weaknesses of its members glossed over. It has all too
often encouraged these weaknesses and suppressed their exposure.
But in this play there is also no question of the Church being
admonished: 'Hands off Science!' Modern science is a legitimate
daughter of the Church, a daughter who has emancipated herself
and turned against the mother.

In the present play the Church functions, even when it op-
poses free research, simply as Authority. Since science was a
branch of theology, the Church is the intellectual authority, the
ultimate, scientific court of appeal. But it is also the temporal
authority, the ultimate political court of appeal. The play shows
the temporary victory of Authority, not the victory of the priesthood. It corresponds to the historical truth in that the Galileo
of the play never turns directly against the Church. There is not
a sentence uttered by Galileo in that sense. If there had been,
such a thorough commission of investigation as the Inquisition
would undoubtedly have brought it to light. And it equally corresponds to the historical truth that the greatest astronomer of the
Papal Roman College, Christopher Clavius, confirmed Galileo's
discoveries (Scene 6). It is also true that clerics were among his
pupils (Scenes 8, 9 and 13).

To take satirical aim at the worldly interests of high dignitaries
seems to me cheap (it would be in Scene 7). But the casual way

in which these high officials treat the physicist is only meant to
show that, by reason of their past experiences, they think they
can count on ready complaisance from Galileo. They are not
mistaken.

Considering our bourgeois politicians, one cannot but extol
the spiritual (and scientific) interests of those politicians of old.

The play, therefore, ignores the falsifications made to the
protocol of 1616 by the Inquisition of 1633, falsifications established by recent historical studies made under the direction of the
German scholar Emil Wohlwill. Doubtless the judgment and
sentence of 1633 were thereby made juridically possible. Any-
body who understands the point of view outlined above will
appreciate that the author was not concerned with this legal side
of the trial. There is no doubt that Urban VIII was personally
incensed at Galileo and, in the most detestable manner, played
an actual part in the proceedings against him. The play passes
this over.

Anyone who understands the standpoint of the author will
appreciate that this attitude implies no reverence for the Church
of the seventeenth, let alone of the twentieth century.

Casting the Church as the embodiment of Authority in this
theatrical trial of the persecutors of the champions of free research certainly does not help to secure an acquittal for the
Church. But it would be highly dangerous, particularly nowadays, to treat a matter like Galileo's fight for freedom of research
as a religious one; for thereby attention would be most unhappily
deflected from present-day reactionary authorities of a totally
unecclesiastical kind.

LAUGHTON'S GALILEO

The novelty of Galileo in his day was brought out by Laughton
letting him gaze with a stranger's eyes at the world around him,
as if it were something requiring an explanation. His laughing
observation of the monks in the Collegium Romanum made fossils
of them. Here, incidentally, he displayed pleasure in their primi-
tive argumentation.

A few people raised objections to L. delivering the first-scene speech about the new astronomy with his torso bare; they said the public might be confused by hearing such intellectual utterances from a half-naked man. But just that very mixture of spiritual and physical interested L. 'Galileo's physical pleasure', when the boy rubbed his back, was transmuted into intellectual creativeness. Thus L. emphasised that Galileo is once more enjoying his wine when, in Scene 9, he hears that the reactionary Pope lies dying. His relaxed way of walking up and down, and the play of his hands in his breeches pockets when planning new researches, verged on the shocking. Whenever Galileo is in a creative mood, L. displayed a contradictory mixture of aggressiveness and defenceless softness and vulnerability.

NOTES

1. The stage decor must not be such that the public believes itself to be in a room in mediaeval Italy or in the Vatican. The public must remain always clearly aware that it is in a theatre.

2. The background should show more than Galileo's immediate surroundings; in an imaginative and artistically attractive way it should show the historical ambience. But it must nevertheless remain a background. (This result will be achieved if the decor, for example, does not obtrude itself with vivid colours, but rather sets off the costumes of the actors and intensifies the plasticity of the figures by itself remaining two-dimensional – even though it contains an element of plasticity, etc.)

3. Furniture and props should be realistic (including doors) and, particularly, should have social-historical charm. The costumes must be individualised and show signs of having been worn. Social distinctions must be emphasised, since we cannot easily recognise them from such old fashions. The colours of the costume should harmonise with one another.

4. The groupings of the characters must have the quality of historical paintings (not in order to bring out the historical element as an aesthetic pleasure; this instruction is equally applicable to contemporary plays). The producer can achieve this by imagining historical titles for the actions. (Example – something like the following for the first scene: '*The physicist Galileo explains*

*the new Copernican System to his future collaborator, Andrea Sarti,
and predicts a great historical importance for astronomy.' – 'In
order to earn his living, the great Galileo teaches rich pupils.' –
'Galileo, who has applied for the means to help him to continue his
studies, is exhorted by the university authorities to invent profitable
instruments.' – 'In the light of a traveller's reports, Galileo constructs
his first telescope.')*

5. The actions must be carried through smoothly and with
detailed forethought. Incessant changes of position by trivial
movements of the characters must be avoided. The producer
must not for a moment forget that many of the actions and
speeches are hard to understand, so that it is necessary to express
the basic meaning of the action through the positions taken up
by the characters. The audience must be sure that someone walking, someone standing up, a gesture, all have meaning and deserve
attention. The grouping and movements must, however, remain
absolutely natural and realistic.

6. The casting of the church dignitaries must be done particularly realistically. No kind of caricature of the Church is intended;
however, the elaborate phraseology and 'culture' of the princes of
the Church of the seventeenth century must not mislead the producer into choosing 'spiritual' types. In this play the Church
represents chiefly Authority; as types the dignitaries of the Church
should resemble our present-day bankers and senators.

7. The characterisation of Galileo should not aim at establish-
ing the sympathetic identification and participation of the audience
with him; rather, the audience should be helped to achieve a more
considering, critical and appraising attitude. He should be presented as a phenomenon, rather like Richard III, whereby the
audience's emotional acceptance is gained through the vitality of
this alien manifestation.

8. The more deeply the historical seriousness of a production
is established, the more freely can rein be given to humour; the
more grandiose the scale of the production, the more intimately
can the scenes be played.

9. Strictly speaking, *The Life of Galileo* can, without much
adjustment of the contemporary theatrical style, be presented as

a piece of historical 'ham' with a star part. A conventional production (which, however, need never consciously strike the per-
formers as conventional, particularly if it contains some original
ideas) must, nevertheless, perceptibly weaken the real power of
the play, without providing the audience with 'easier access'. The
most important effects of the play would misfire if the 'contemporary theatre' did not make the necessary adjustment.

The answer: 'That won't work here', is familiar to the author;
he heard it at home, too. Most producers treat plays like this, as
a coachman would a motor car when it was first invented. On
the arrival of the machine, mistrusting the practical instructions
accompanying it, this coachman would have harnessed horses in
front – more horses, of course, than to a carriage, since the new
car was heavier – and then, his attention being drawn to the engine,
he too would have said: 'That won't work here.'

The Life of Galileo

COLLABORATOR: M. Steffin

MUSIC: Hanns Eisler

TRANSLATOR: Desmond I. Vesey

Written in 1938–39 and 1945–47. First produced in the Zurich
Schauspielhaus on 9 September 1943

CHARACTERS

*Galileo Galilei: Andrea Sarti: Signora Sarti, Galileo's house-
keeper and Andrea's mother: Ludovico Marsili, a rich young man:
the Curator of the University of Padua, Signor Priuli: Sagredo,
Galileo's friend: Virginia, Galileo's daughter: Federzoni, a lens-
grinder, Galileo's collaborator: the Doge: senators: Cosimo de'
Medici, Grand Duke of Florence: the Court Chamberlain: the
theologian: the philosopher: the mathematician: the older court
lady: the younger court lady: the Grand Duke's lackey: two nuns:
two soldiers: the old lady: a fat prelate: two scholars: two monks:
two astronomers: a very thin monk: the very old cardinal: Father
Christopher Clavius, astronomer: the little monk: the Cardinal
Inquisitor: Cardinal Barberini, later Pope Urban VIII: Cardinal
Bellarmin: two ecclesiastical secretaries: two young ladies: Filippo
Mucius, a scholar: Signor Gaffone, Rector of the University of
Pisa: the ballad-singer: his wife: Vanni, an iron-founder: an
official: a high official: an individual: a monk: a peasant: a frontier
guard: a scribe: men, women, children.*

GALILEO GALILEI, TEACHER OF MATHEMATICS AT PADUA, DETERMINES TO PROVE THE NEW COPERNICAN SYSTEM

In the year sixteen hundred and nine
Science's light began to shine.
At Padua City, in a modest house
Galileo Galilei set out to prove
The sun is still, the earth is on the move.

Galileo's humble Study in Padua

It is morning. A boy, Andrea, the son of the housekeeper, brings in a glass of milk and a roll of bread.

GALILEO *washing the upper part of his body, puffing, and good-humoured*: Put the milk on the table. But don't shut any of my books.

ANDREA: Mother says we must pay the milkman. If we don't, he'll soon be taking a circle round our house, Signor Galilei.

GALILEO: The expression is: he will be *describing* a circle, Andrea.

ANDREA: All right. If we don't pay, he'll be describing a circle round us, Signor Galilei.

GALILEO: While the bailiff, Signor Cambione, will come straight here by taking what sort of a line between two points?

ANDREA *grinning*: The shortest.

GALILEO: Good. I've got something for you. Look behind the star-charts.

Andrea fishes out from behind the star-charts a large wooden model of the Ptolemaic system.

ANDREA: What is it?

GALILEO: That shows how, according to the ancients, the stars move round the earth.

ANDREA: How?

GALILEO: Let's examine it. Begin at the beginning: description.

ANDREA: In the middle is a little stone.

GALILEO: That is the earth.

ANDREA: Then all around, one outside the other, there are globes.

GALILEO: How many?

ANDREA: Eight.

GALILEO: Those are the crystal spheres.

ANDREA: And the globes have little balls fixed on ...

GALILEO: The stars.

ANDREA: There are strips with words painted on them.

GALILEO: What words?

ANDREA: The names of stars.

GALILEO: Such as?

ANDREA: The lowest ball is the moon, it's written on it. And above it is the sun.

GALILEO: And now make the sun move.

ANDREA *moves the globes*: That's beautiful. But we're so shut in.

GALILEO *drying himself*: Yes, I felt that too when I saw the thing for the first time. Some people do feel it. *He throws the towel to Andrea, for him to dry his back.* Walls and globes and immobility! For two thousand years men have believed that the sun and all the stars of heaven revolve about them. The pope, the cardinals, the princes, the scholars, captains, merchants, fishwives and schoolboys believed themselves to be sitting motionless in the centre of this crystal globe. But now we are travelling headlong into space, Andrea. For the old age is past, and this is a new age. During the last hundred years it has been as though men were expecting something.

The cities are narrow and so are men's minds. Superstition and plague. But now we say: because it is so, it will not remain so. For everything moves, my boy.

I like to think that it began with ships. Ever since men could remember they crept only along the coasts; then suddenly they left the coasts and sped straight out across the seas.

On our old continent a rumour started: there are new continents! And since our ships have been sailing to them the word has gone round all the laughing continents that the vast, dreaded ocean is just a little pond. And a great desire has arisen to fathom the causes of all things: why a stone falls when you drop it, and how it rises when you throw it in the air. Every day something new is discovered. Even centenarians let the youngsters shout the latest novelty into their ears.

Already much has been discovered, but there is more still to be found out. And so there are always new things for new generations to do.

When a young man in Siena, I saw how a couple of builders, after five minutes argument, replaced a thousand-year-old system for moving granite blocks by a new and more practical arrangement of the tackle. Then and there I knew – the old age is past and a new age is here. Soon mankind will know the truth about their home, about the heavenly body on which they dwell. What is written in the old books no longer satisfies them.

For where belief has prevailed for a thousand years, doubt now prevails. All the world says: yes, that's written in books but now let us see for ourselves. The most solemn truths are being tapped on the shoulder; what was never doubted is now in doubt.

And because of that a great wind has arisen, lifting even the gold-embroidered coat-tails of princes and prelates, so that the fat legs and thin legs underneath are seen; legs like our legs. The heavens, it has turned out, are empty. And there is a gale of laughter over that.

But the waters of the earth are driving our new spindles and in the dockyard, in the rope and sail shops, five hundred hands are moving together in a new way of working.

I predict that in our lifetimes astronomy will be talked about in the market-places. Even the sons of fishwives will go to school. For these city people seeking after novelty will be glad that the new astronomy now lets the earth move freely, too. It has always been said that the stars are affixed to a crystal sphere to prevent them falling down. But now we have plucked up courage and we let them soar through space, unfettered and in full career, like our ships, unfettered and in full career.

And the earth rolls happily round the sun, and the fish-wives, merchants, princes and cardinals and even the Pope roll with it.

Overnight the universe has lost its centre, and by morning it has countless ones. So that now each – and none – is regarded as its centre. For suddenly there is plenty of room.

Our ships sail far across the seas, our stars travel far through space; even in chess the castles have lately taken to moving all over the board.

What does the poet say? 'Oh happy morning of beginning . . .'

ANDREA: 'Oh happy morning of beginning!
            Oh scent of winds from new and distant shores!'
And you must drink your milk; for people will start coming again soon.

GALILEO: Do you understand what I told you yesterday?

ANDREA: What? All that about Kippernicus and his rotation?

GALILEO: Yes.

ANDREA: No. How do you expect me to understand it? It's very difficult, and I'm only eleven next October.

GALILEO: I particularly want *you* to understand it too. That's why I'm working and buying expensive books instead of paying the milkman – so that people like you can understand it.

ANDREA: But I can *see* that the sun is in a different place in the evening from what it was in the morning. So it can't be standing still. Never, never.

GALILEO: You *see*! What do you see? You see nothing. You only goggle. Goggling is not seeing. *He sets the iron wash-basin in the middle of the room.* Well, that's the sun. Sit down. *Andrea sits on the one chair. Galileo stands behind him.* Where is the sun, right or left?

ANDREA: Left.

GALILEO: And how can it get to your right?

ANDREA: If you carry it to the right, of course.

GALILEO: Is that the only way? *He picks him up with the chair and rotates him through a semicircle.* Now where is the sun?

ANDREA: On the right.

GALILEO: And did it move?

ANDREA: No! *It* didn't.

GALILEO: Well, what did move?

ANDREA: I did.

GALILEO *shouts*: Wrong, you idiot! The chair.

ANDREA: But I went with it!

GALILEO: Of course you did. The chair is the earth. You are sitting on it.

SIGNORA SARTI *has entered to make the bed. She has been looking on*: Whatever are you doing with my boy, Signor Galilei?

GALILEO: I'm teaching him to see, Sarti.

SIGNORA SARTI: By lugging him round the room?

ANDREA: Stop it, mother. You don't understand this.

SIGNORA SARTI: Don't I? But you understand it, eh? – A young gentleman wishing tuition. Very well dressed and brings a letter of recommendation. *She hands this over.* You'll soon have my Andrea saying twice two is five. He already muddles up everything you tell him. Yesterday evening he actually was proving to me that the earth goes round the sun. He is firmly convinced that a gentleman by the name of Kippernicus has worked that out.

ANDREA: Didn't Kippernicus work it out, Signor Galilei? Tell her yourself.

SIGNORA SARTI: What! Are you really teaching him such nonsense? So that he'll chatter about it at school and the reverend gentlemen will come complaining to me because he repeats all this unholy stuff. You ought to be ashamed of yourself, Signor Galilei.

GALILEO *breakfasting*: As a result of our investigations, Signora Sarti, and after bitter dispute, Andrea and I have made discoveries which we can no longer withhold from the world. A new era has dawned, a great age in which it is a joy to be alive.

SIGNORA SARTI: Well! I hope we shall also be able to pay the milkman in this new age, Signor Galilei. *Pointing to the letter of recommendation.* Just do me one favour and don't send *him* away too. I'm thinking of the milk bill.

Exit.

GALILEO *laughing*: At least let me finish my milk! *To Andrea*: So we did understand something yesterday, after all!

ANDREA: I only said it to her to astonish her. But it isn't true. When I was in the chair, you only turned it round – and not like that. *He makes a vertically circular movement with his arm.* Because if you had done that I should have fallen off, and that's a fact. Why didn't you turn the chair upside down? Because then it would have proved that I should also fall off the earth if it turned like that. There you are!

GALILEO: But I have proved to you . . .

ANDREA: But last night I discovered that if the earth really turned like that I'd be hanging head downwards at night. And that's a fact.

GALILEO *taking an apple from the table*: Look, this is the earth.

ANDREA: Don't take examples like that, Signor Galilei. You can prove anything with them.

GALILEO *putting the apple back*: All right.

ANDREA: You can do anything with examples if you're clever enough. Only I can't lug my mother about in a chair like you did me. So you see what a bad example that is. And what about it, if the apple *is* the earth? That's nothing.

GALILEO *laughs*: You don't want to know.

ANDREA: Pick it up again. Why don't I hang head downwards at night?

GALILEO: Well, here is the earth, and this is you standing on it. *He sticks a splinter from a piece of kindling wood into the apple.* And now the earth rotates.

ANDREA: And now I'm hanging head downwards.

GALILEO: How? Look carefully. Where is your head?

ANDREA *points at the apple*: There. Down below.

GALILEO: What? *He turns the apple back.* Isn't your head in the same place? Aren't your feet still on the ground? Are you like this when I turn it?

He takes the splinter out and turns it upside down.

ANDREA: No. Then why don't I feel the earth turning?

GALILEO: Because you're turning with it. You and the air around you and everything that's on the globe.

ANDREA: And why does it look as if the sun's moving?

GALILEO *once more rotates the apple with the splinter in it*: Now, below you you see the earth, that stays the same, it's always below you and never moves so far as you are concerned. But now look above you. Now the lamp is over your head. But now, when I've turned the earth, what's over your head now – that is, up above?

ANDREA *rotates himself too*: The stove.

GALILEO: And where is the lamp?

ANDREA: Down below.

GALILEO: There you are!

ANDREA: That's fine. That'll amaze her!

Ludovico Marsili, a rich young man, enters.

GALILEO: This place is like a cross-roads.

LUDOVICO: Good morning, signor. My name is Ludovico Marsili.

GALILEO *studying his letter of recommendation*: You have been in Holland?

LUDOVICO: Where I heard much of you, Signor Galilei.

GALILEO: Your family owns estates in the Campagna?

LUDOVICO: My mother wants me to have a look round. See what's happening in the world, and so on.

GALILEO: And you heard in Holland that I, for example, was happening in Italy?

LUDOVICO: And since my mother wishes me to have a look round in the world of science too . . .

GALILEO: Private tuition, ten scudi a month.

LUDOVICO: Very well, signor.

GALILEO: What are your interests?

LUDOVICO: Horses.

GALILEO: Ah.

LUDOVICO: I have no head for learning, Signor Galilei.

GALILEO: Indeed. In that case it will be fifteen scudi a month.

LUDOVICO: Very well, Signor Galilei.

GALILEO: I shall have to take you early in the morning. That will be your loss, Andrea. For of course you'll have to drop out. You understand; *you* don't pay.

ANDREA: All right, I'm going. Can I have the apple?

GALILEO: Yes.

Exit Andrea.

LUDOVICO: You will have to have patience with me. Particularly since in science everything is different from what plain commonsense tells one. You take for example that funny tube they're selling in Amsterdam. I examined it closely. Just a casing of green leather and two lenses, one like that – *he indicates by gesture a concave lens* – and one like that – *he indicates a convex lens.* I hear that one enlarges and the other diminishes. Any sensible person would think that they'd cancel each other out. Wrong. One sees everything five times as large through the thing. That's your science for you.

GALILEO: What does one see five times as large?

LUDOVICO: Church spires, doves; everything that's far away.

GALILEO: Have you yourself seen church spires enlarged like that?

LUDOVICO: Yes, signor.

GALILEO: And the tube had two lenses? *He makes a sketch on a piece of paper.* Did it look like that? *Ludovico nods.* How old is this discovery?

LUDOVICO: I don't think it was more than a few days old when I left Holland; in any case it hadn't been longer on the market.

GALILEO *almost friendly*: And why must it be physics? Why not horse-breeding?

Enter Signora Sarti, unnoticed by Galileo.

LUDOVICO: My mother thinks that a little science is necessary. All the world takes a drop of science with their wine nowadays, you know.

GALILEO: You could just as well choose a dead language or theology. That's easier. *He sees Signora Sarti.* All right, come on Tuesday morning.

Exit Ludovico.

GALILEO: Don't look at me like that. I've accepted him.

SIGNORA SARTI: Because you saw me at the right moment. The Curator of the University is outside.

GALILEO: Bring him in, he's important. It may mean five hundred scudi. Then I won't need any pupils.

Signora Sarti brings in the Curator. Galileo has finished dressing and is scribbling figures on a scrap of paper.

Good morning, lend me half a scudo. *He gives the coin, which the Curator digs out of his purse, to Sarti.* Sarti, send Andrea down to the spectacles-maker for two lenses; here are the particulars.

Exit Sarti with the note.

THE CURATOR: I have called respecting your application for an increase in salary to a thousand scudi. Unfortunately, I cannot recommend this to the University. You know that at the present time the mathematical faculty is no attraction at a university. Mathematics is a profitless art, so to speak. Not that the Republic does not esteem it most highly. It is not as necessary as philosophy, nor as useful as theology, but it affords its devotees such endless pleasures.

GALILEO *over his papers*: My dear man, I cannot manage on five hundred scudi.

THE CURATOR: But Signor Galilei! You lecture twice a week, two hours at a time. Your exceptional reputation must surely bring you as many pupils as you wish, all of whom can pay for private lessons. Have you no private pupils?

GALILEO: Sir, I have too many! I teach and teach, and when have I time to study? God above, I am not as omniscient as the gentlemen of the philosophic faculty. I am stupid. I understand absolutely nothing. So I am compelled to patch up the holes in my knowledge. And when am I to do that?

When am I to research? Sir, my science is still hungry for knowledge! For the answers to our greatest problems, we have so far nothing but hypotheses. And *we* demand proofs. But how can I progress when, to keep my household going, I am driven to drum into any blockhead who can pay the fact that parallel lines meet at infinity?

THE CURATOR: You should not altogether forget that, while the Republic may not pay as much as certain Princes do, it guarantees freedom of research. We in Padua admit even Protestants to our lectures! And we grant them doctorates. Not only did we not surrender Signor Cremonini to the Inquisition when it was proved to us – *proved*, Signor Galilei – that he gives vent to irreligious utterances, but we even voted him a higher salary. As far away as Holland it is known that Venice is the republic where the Inquisition has no say. And that is worth something to you who are an astronomer – that is, devoting yourself to a science which has for a considerable time ceased to show a due respect for the teachings of the Church!

GALILEO: Your people here handed Signor Giordano Bruno over to the authorities in Rome. Because he spread the teachings of Copernicus.

THE CURATOR: Not because he spread the teachings of Copernicus, which are moreover false, but because he was not a Venetian and also had no appointment here. So you can leave out of your argument this man who was burnt at the stake. By the way, for all our freedom you would be well advised not to utter so loudly a name on which the Church has laid its anathema. Not even here, Signor Galilei. Not even here.

GALILEO: Your protection of freedom of thought is quite a profitable business, eh? By pointing out that elsewhere the Inquisition rules and burns, you get good teachers cheap. In return for protection from the Inquisition you reimburse yourselves by paying the worst salaries.

THE CURATOR: Unjust! Unjust! What good would it do you to have all the free time in the world for your researches if every ignorant monk of the Inquisition could simply forbid your thoughts? No rose without a thorn, no princes without monks, Signor Galilei.

GALILEO: And what use is freedom of research without free time in which to research? What happens to the results? Perhaps you would care to show the gentlemen of the Signoria these investigations into the Laws of Falling Bodies – *he points to a bundle of manuscripts* – and ask them whether that is not worth a few more scudi?

THE CURATOR: It is worth infinitely more, Signor Galilei.

GALILEO: Not infinitely more, but five hundred scudi more, sir.

THE CURATOR: Scudi are worth what scudi will buy. If you want money, you must produce something else. For the knowledge which you sell, you can only demand as much as it profits whoever buys it from you. For example, the philosophy which Signor Colombe is selling in Florence brings the Prince at least ten thousand scudi a year. Your Laws of Falling Bodies have created a stir, admittedly. Men applaud you in Paris and Prague. But the gentlemen who applaud there do not, unfortunately, pay the University of Padua what you cost it. Your misfortune is your subject, Signor Galilei.

GALILEO: I understand. Free trade, free research. Free trading in research, eh?

THE CURATOR: But, Signor Galilei! What a suggestion! Permit me to say that I do not understand your jesting remarks. The flourishing trade of the Republic seems to me to be scarcely a subject for derision. Even less could I, for so many years Curator of the University, bring myself to speak of research in that – may I say – frivolous tone. *As Galileo casts longing glances at his work-table.* Consider the conditions in the world outside: the whips of bondage under which learning groans in certain places – whips which the authorities have cut from their old leather folios. In those places people must not know how a stone falls, only what Aristotle writes on the subject. Eyes are just for reading. What need for new laws of falling bodies, where only the laws of a footfall are important? Set against that the endless pleasure with which our Republic accepts your ideas, however daring they may be. Here you can research. Here you can work. No one supervises you, no one oppresses you. Our merchants, who appreciate the importance of better linen in their struggle against Florentine competition, listen with interest to your call for better physics; and how greatly is the science of physics indebted to the call for better looms! Our most eminent citizens interest themselves in your researches, visit you, watch demonstrations of your discoveries, and they are gentlemen whose time is precious. Do not despise trade, Signor Galilei! No one here would tolerate your work being disturbed in the slightest degree or that intruders should make difficulties for you. Admit, Signor Galilei, that you can work here.

GALILEO *in desperation*: Yes.

THE CURATOR: And as far as the material side is concerned, why don't you invent something else as pretty as your wonderful proportional compasses which – *he counts off on his fingers* – enable one without any mathematical knowledge to protract lines, calculate compound interest on capital, reproduce ground plans in varying scales, and determine the weight of cannon-balls.

GALILEO: A toy!

THE CURATOR: Something that has delighted and amazed the highest in the Republic and also brought in cash, you call a toy. I hear that even General Stefano Gritti is able to extract square roots with this instrument.

GALILEO: Indeed a miracle! – Nevertheless, Priuli, you have made me thoughtful. Priuli, perhaps I have something of the sort you mentioned. *He picks up the paper with the sketch on it.*

THE CURATOR: Have you? That would be the solution. *He stands up.* Signor Galilei, we know that you are a great man. A great but discontented man, if I may say so.

GALILEO: Yes, I am discontented, and *that* is what you would pay me for, if you had the wit! For I am discontented with myself. But instead of that you force me to be discontented with you. I admit that it amuses me to prove my worth to you gentlemen of Venice, in your famous arsenal and your dockyards and your cannon foundries. But you leave me no time to pursue the far-reaching speculations on my own subject which crowd into my mind when I am there. You muzzle the ox which threshes! I am forty-six years old and have done nothing which satisfies me.

THE CURATOR: Then let me disturb you no longer.

GALILEO: Thank you.

Exit the Curator. Galileo, alone for a few moments, starts to work. Then Andrea comes running in.

GALILEO *working*: Why haven't you eaten the apple?

ANDREA: So that I could show her that it turns.

GALILEO: I must say something to you, Andrea. Don't talk to other people about our ideas.

ANDREA: Why not?

GALILEO: The authorities have forbidden them.

ANDREA: But they're the truth.

GALILEO: But they forbid them. In this case there is something else as well. We physicists still cannot prove what we believe to be correct. Even the teaching of the great Copernicus has not yet been proved. It is only a hypothesis. Give me the lenses.

ANDREA: The half scudo wasn't enough. I had to leave my coat behind. Pledge.

GALILEO: What will you do in winter without a coat?

A pause. Galileo arranges the lenses on the sheet of paper bearing the sketch.

ANDREA: What is a hypothesis?

GALILEO: It is when one accepts something as probable, but has no facts. That Signora Felice down the street by the basketmaker's shop, who has a child at the breast, gives the baby milk and doesn't take milk from it, is a hypothesis until one goes and sees it and can prove it to be a fact. But in dealing with the stars we are like worms with clouded eyes who can see only very little. The old teachings, which were believed for a thousand years, are collapsing; there is less wood in those gigantic structures than in the props that are supposed to shore them up – the many laws that explain little. Whereas this new hypothesis has few laws that explain much.

ANDREA: But you have proved everything to me.

GALILEO: Only that it *can* be so. You understand, the hypothesis is a very fine one, and there is nothing against it.

ANDREA: I should like to be a physicist too, Signor Galilei.

GALILEO: I believe it – seeing the infinity of questions to be cleared up in our field. *He has crossed to the window and looked through the lenses. Mildly interested* : Take a look through this, Andrea.

ANDREA: Holy Mary, everything comes close. The bell on the campanile is quite near. I can even read the copper letters: Gratia Dei.

GALILEO: That will bring us in five hundred scudi.

2

GALILEO PRESENTS THE REPUBLIC OF VENICE
WITH A NEW DISCOVERY

No one's virtue is complete:
Great Galileo likes to eat.
You will not resent, we hope,
The truth about his telescope.

The Great Arsenal of Venice, by the Harbour

Senators, at their head the Doge. To one side, Galileo's friend Sagredo and fifteen-year-old Virginia Galileo with a velvet cushion on which lies a telescope which is about two foot long and covered with crimson leather. On a dais, Galileo. Behind him the stand for the telescope, attended by Federzoni, the lens-grinder.

GALILEO: Your Excellency, noble Signoria! As a teacher of mathematics at your University of Padua and director of your great arsenal here in Venice, I have always regarded it as my duty not only to fulfil my high responsibility of teaching, but also to provide especial benefits for the Republic of Venice by means of practical discoveries. With deep pleasure and all due humility I am able to display and present to you here today a completely new instrument, my distance-glass or telescope, produced in your world-famous Great Arsenal according to the highest scientific and Christian principles, the fruit of seventeen years patient research by your obedient servant.

Galileo leaves the dais and takes up position beside Sagredo. Clapping. Galileo bows.

GALILEO *softly to Sagredo*: Waste of time!

SAGREDO *softly*: You'll be able to pay your butcher, my friend.

GALILEO: Yes, it will bring them in money. *He bows again.*

THE CURATOR *stepping on to the dais*: Excellency, noble Signoria! Once again a page of fame in the great books of the arts is embellished with Venetian characters. *Polite applause.* A scholar of world repute here presents to you, and you alone, a highly saleable cylinder to manufacture and put on the market in any way you please. *Stronger applause.* And has it occurred to you that in war-time by means of this instrument we shall be able to distinguish the build and number of an enemy's ships a full two hours earlier than he can descry ours, so that we, knowing his strength, can decide whether to pursue in order to give battle or to fly? *Very loud applause.* And now, Your Excellency, noble Signoria, Signor Galilei begs you to receive this instrument of his own inventing, this testimony to his intuition, from the hands of his charming daughter.

Music. Virginia advances, bows, and presents the telescope to the Curator, who passes it on to Federzoni. Federzoni places it on the stand and adjusts it. The Doge and senators climb on to the dais and peer through the telescope.

GALILEO *softly*: I can't promise you that I shall be able to last out this carnival. These people here think that they're getting a profitable toy; but it's far more. I pointed the tube at the moon last night.

SAGREDO: What did you see?

GALILEO: It has no light of its own.

SAGREDO: What?

SENATORS: I can see the fortifications of Santa Rosita, Signor Galilei! – On that boat over there they're having their midday meal. Grilled fish. It makes my mouth water.

GALILEO: I tell you, astronomy has stood still for a thousand years because they had no telescope.

SENATOR: Signor Galilei!

SAGREDO: They're speaking to you.

SENATOR: One sees too well with that thing. I'll have to tell my womankind that bathing on the roof won't do any more.

GALILEO: Do you know what the Milky Way consists of?

SAGREDO: No.

SENATOR: One could easily ask ten scudi for a thing like that, Signor Galilei.

Galileo bows.

VIRGINIA *bringing Ludovico to her father*: Ludovico wants to congratulate you, father.

LUDOVICO *embarrassed*: I congratulate you, sir.

GALILEO: I have improved it.

LUDOVICO: Of course, sir. I see you have made the cover red; in Holland it was green.

GALILEO *turning to Sagredo*: I'm just wondering whether with this thing I may not be able to prove a certain theory.

SAGREDO: Take care.

THE CURATOR: Your five hundred scudi are safe and sure, Signor Galilei.

GALILEO *paying no attention to him*: Of course I am very wary of drawing any premature conclusion.

The Doge, a fat, unassuming man, has come up to Galileo and is trying with clumsy dignity to speak to him.

THE CURATOR: Signor Galilei, his Excellency the Doge.

The Doge shakes Galileo's hand.

GALILEO: Of course! The five hundred! Are you satisfied, your Excellency?

THE DOGE: Unfortunately, in the Republic we always need a pretext to enable our city fathers to agree to grant anything to our scholars.

THE CURATOR: And for that matter, Signor Galilei, where else would your incentive lie?

THE DOGE *smiling*: We need the pretext.

The Doge and the Curator lead Galileo to the senators, who surround him. Virginia and Ludovico walk slowly away.

VIRGINIA: Did I do it all right?

LUDOVICO: I thought it was all right.

VIRGINIA: What's the matter with you then?

LUDOVICO: Oh, nothing. Perhaps a green cover would have been just as good.

VIRGINIA: I think they are all pleased with father.

LUDOVICO: And I think I'm beginning to understand something about science.

3

10TH JANUARY, 1610: BY MEANS OF THE TELESCOPE GALILEO DISCOVERS PHENOMENA IN THE SKY WHICH PROVE THE COPERNICAN SYSTEM. WARNED BY HIS FRIEND AGAINST THE POSSIBLE CONSEQUENCES OF HIS RESEARCHES, GALILEO PROFESSES HIS BELIEF IN MAN'S REASON.

January ten, sixteen ten:
Galileo Galilei abolishes heaven.

Galileo's Work-Room in Padua

Night. Galileo and Sagredo, wrapped in thick cloaks, at the telescope.

SAGREDO *looking through the telescope, half to himself*: The edge of the crescent is quite uneven, jagged and irregular. In the dark half, near the luminous edge, are luminous spots. They appear one after the other. From these spots the light streams over ever-widening areas until it merges into the greater, luminous part.

GALILEO: How do you explain those luminous spots?

SAGREDO: It cannot be.

GALILEO: But it is. They are mountains.

SAGREDO: On a star?

GALILEO: Giant mountains. Whose summits are gilded by the rising sun, whilst all around night still covers their slopes. You see the light descending from the topmost peaks into the valleys.

SAGREDO: But that contradicts all astronomy for the last two thousand years.

GALILEO: Yet that's how it is. What you see has never been seen by any man besides myself. You are the second.

SAGREDO: The moon cannot be an earth with mountains and valleys, any more than the earth can be a star.

GALILEO: The moon *can* be an earth with mountains and valleys, and the earth *can* be a star. An ordinary heavenly body – one among thousands. Look again. Do you see the darkened part of the moon quite dark?

SAGREDO: No. Now when I look closely I can see a pale, ashen light upon it.

GALILEO: What sort of light could that be?

SAGREDO: ?

GALILEO: It's light from the earth.

SAGREDO: That's nonsense. How can the earth shine – a dead body, with its mountains and forests and seas?

GALILEO: In the same way as the moon shines. Both stars are illuminated by the sun – that is why they shine. What the moon is to us, we are to the moon. Sometimes it sees us as a crescent, and sometimes full, and sometimes not at all.

SAGREDO: So there would be no difference between the moon and the earth?

GALILEO: Evidently not.

SAGREDO: Not ten years ago a man was burnt in Rome. His name was Giordano Bruno, and he alleged just that.

GALILEO: He did. And now we can see it. Keep your eye at the telescope, Sagredo. What you see means that there is no difference between Heaven and Earth. Today is the tenth of

January, sixteen hundred and ten. Mankind will write in its journal: Heaven abolished.

SAGREDO: That is appalling.

GALILEO: I have discovered yet another fact. Perhaps even more astonishing ...

SARTI *enters*: The Curator.

The Curator bursts in.

THE CURATOR: Forgive the lateness of the hour. I should be obliged if I could speak to you alone.

GALILEO: Signor Sagredo can hear anything that I can hear, Signor Priuli.

THE CURATOR: But you may not find it pleasant for the gentleman to hear what has happened. It is, unfortunately, something absolutely incredible.

GALILEO: Signor Sagredo is accustomed to encountering the incredible with me, you know.

THE CURATOR: I fear, I fear. *Pointing to the telescope*. Yes, there it is, that marvellous thing! The thing you might just as well throw away. It's worthless, absolutely worthless.

SAGREDO *who has been wandering around restlessly*: What do you mean?

THE CURATOR: Do you know that this discovery of yours, which you have described as the fruit of seventeen years research, can be bought on any street corner in Italy for a few scudi? And, what is more, made in Holland! At this moment a Dutch cargo ship in the harbour is unloading five hundred telescopes!

GALILEO: Really?

THE CURATOR: I fail to understand your equanimity, Signor.

SAGREDO: What are you worrying about? Let me tell you that in these last few days Signor Galilei, by means of this instrument, has made revolutionary discoveries concerning the universe.

GALILEO *laughing*: You can have a look through it, Priuli.

THE CURATOR: Well, let me tell you that it is quite enough for me – as the man who got Signor Galilei's salary doubled for this trash – to have made *this* discovery. And it is pure coincidence that the gentlemen of the Signoria, believing that they were securing for the Republic an instrument which could only be produced here, did not, the first time they looked through it, perceive at the nearest street corner, seven times enlarged, a common pedlar selling this tube for a song.

Galileo laughs uproariously.

SAGREDO: My dear Signor Priuli, I may not be able to assess this instrument's value to commerce, but its value to philosophy is so incalculable that . . .

THE CURATOR: To philosophy! What has Signor Galilei, the mathematician, to do with philosophy? – Signor Galilei, in your day you have invented an excellent water-pump for the city, and your irrigation plant functions satisfactorily. The cloth-weavers, too, praise your machines. However could I have expected such a thing!

GALILEO: Not so fast, Priuli. Sea passages are still long, uncertain and expensive. We still lack any sort of reliable clock in the sky. Some signpost for navigation. Now, I have reason to believe that with this telescope certain stars which follow very regular courses may be observed clearly. New star-charts could save millions of scudi in navigation, Priuli.

THE CURATOR: Enough, enough. I have already listened to too much from you. In reward for my kindness you have made me the laughing-stock of the city. I shall always be remembered as the Curator who was taken in by a worthless spyglass. You have every reason to laugh. You have your five hundred scudi. But I can tell you – and it is an honest man speaking – this world disgusts me!

Exit, slamming the door behind him.

GALILEO: In his rage he becomes almost likeable. Did you hear that: a world where there are no bargains to be made disgusts him!

SAGREDO: Had you known about these Dutch instruments?

GALILEO: Of course, from hearsay. But I constructed one twice as good for those signorial money-bags. How can I work with a bailiff in the room? And Virginia will certainly be needing a dowry soon. She's not intelligent. And then, I like to buy books – not only about physics – and I like to eat decently. It's when I'm eating that I get most inspiration. A rotten age! They haven't paid me as much as the man who drives their wine-carts. Four cords of kindling wood for two lectures on mathematics. I have now extracted five hundred scudi from them, but I still have debts, some of them twenty years old. Five years respite for research, and I should have proved everything. – Now I will show you something else.

SAGREDO *hesitates to approach the telescope*: I have a feeling very like fear, Galileo.

GALILEO: I am now going to show you one of the shining, milk-white clouds of the Galaxy. Tell me what it is composed of.

SAGREDO: Those are stars. Countless stars.

GALILEO: In the constellations of Orion alone there are five hundred fixed stars. Those are the many worlds, the numberless others, the further stars of which Giordano spoke. He did not see them; he predicted them.

SAGREDO: But even if the earth is a star, that's still a long way from the assertions of Copernicus that it revolves round the sun. There is no star in Heaven round which another one revolves. Except that the moon revolves round the earth.

GALILEO: Sagredo, I have been wondering. Since the day before yesterday I have been wondering. There is Jupiter. *He focuses on it.* There are four smaller stars close by it, which you can only see through the telescope. I saw them on Monday, but took no particular notice of their position. Yesterday I looked again. I could have sworn that all four had changed their position. I made a note of it. Now their position is different again. What's this? I saw four. *Excitedly*: Look! Look!

SAGREDO: I see three.

GALILEO: Where is the fourth? Here are the tables. We must calculate what movements they could have made.

They set to work excitedly. It grows dark on the stage, but on the circular horizon Jupiter and its satellites are still visible. When it

*becomes light again, Galileo and Sagredo are still sitting there, with
their winter cloaks on.*

GALILEO: It is proved. The fourth can only have gone behind
   Jupiter, where it cannot be seen. There you have a star round
   which another revolves.

SAGREDO: But the crystal sphere to which Jupiter is attached?

GALILEO: Yes, where is it now? How can Jupiter be attached to
   anything when other stars circle round it? There is no frame-
   work in Heaven, there is no fixity in the universe. There is
   another sun!

SAGREDO: Calm yourself. You think too quickly.

GALILEO: Quickly! Rouse yourself, man! What you have seen,
   no one has seen before. – They were right.

SAGREDO: Who? The Copernicans?

GALILEO: And the others! The whole world was against them,
   and they were right. This is something for Andrea! *Beside
   himself with excitement, he runs to the door and shouts*: Signora
   Sarti! Signora Sarti!

SAGREDO: Galileo, calm yourself!

GALILEO: Sagredo, excite yourself! Signora Sarti!

SAGREDO *turns the telescope away*: Will you stop roaring around
   like a lunatic?

GALILEO: And will you stop standing there like a cod-fish – when
   the truth has been discovered.

SAGREDO: I am not standing like a cod-fish, but I tremble lest it
   may in fact be the truth.

GALILEO: What?

SAGREDO: Have you entirely lost your senses? Do you really no
   longer know what you are involved in, if what you see there
   is true? And you go shouting about for all the world to hear:
   that the earth is a star and not the centre of the universe.

GALILEO: Yes! And that the whole, vast universe with all its stars
   does not revolve round our tiny earth – as must be obvious to
   everyone.

SAGREDO: So that there are only stars there! – And where then is
   God?

GALILEO: What do you mean?

SAGREDO: God! Where is God?

GALILEO *angrily*: Not there! Any more than he could be found on earth, if there were beings up there and they were to seek him here!

SAGREDO: Then where *is* God?

GALILEO: Am I a theologian? I'm a mathematician.

SAGREDO: First and foremost, you are a man. And I ask you, where is God in your universe?

GALILEO: In us or nowhere.

SAGREDO *shouting*: As the heretic Giordano said?

GALILEO: As the heretic Giordano said.

SAGREDO: That was why he was burnt! Not ten years ago!

GALILEO: Because he could prove nothing. Because he only stated it. – Signora Sarti!

SAGREDO: Galileo, I have always regarded you as a shrewd man. For seventeen years in Padua and for three years in Pisa you patiently instructed hundreds of pupils in the Ptolemaic system which the Church supports and the Scriptures, on which the Church is founded, confirm. You thought it untrue, like Copernicus; but you taught it.

GALILEO: Because I could *prove* nothing.

SAGREDO *incredulously*: And you believe that makes a difference?

GALILEO: All the difference in the world! Look here, Sagredo. I believe in mankind, and that means I believe in its commonsense. Without that belief I should not have the strength to get up from my bed in the morning.

SAGREDO: Then I will tell you something. I do *not* believe in it. Forty years among men has consistently taught me that they are not amenable to commonsense. Show them the red tail of a comet, fill them with black terror, and they will all come running out of their houses and break their legs. But tell them one sensible proposition, and support it with seven reasons, and they will simply laugh in your face.

GALILEO: That is untrue – and a slander. I cannot understand how you, believing such a thing, can yet love science. Only the dead are no longer moved by reason.

SAGREDO: How can you confuse their miserable cunning with reason?

GALILEO: I am not speaking of their cunning. I know they call a donkey a horse when they want to sell, and a horse a donkey when they want to buy. That is their cunning. The old woman who, on the eve of a journey, gives her mule an extra bundle of hay with her horny hand; the mariner who, when laying in stores, thinks of storms and calms ahead; the child who pulls on his cap when it is proved to him that it may rain – they are my hope – they all listen to reason. Yes, I believe in the gentle power of reason, of commonsense, over men. They cannot resist it in the long run. No man can watch for long and see how I – *he lets fall a stone from his hand to the floor* – drop a stone, and then say: 'It does not fall.' No man is capable of that. The temptation offered by such a proof is too great. Most succumb to it, and in the long run – all. Thinking is one of the greatest pleasures of the human race.

SIGNORA SARTI *enters*: Do you want something, Signor Galilei?

GALILEO *who is again at his telescope making notes, very amiably*: Yes, I want Andrea.

SIGNORA SARTI: Andrea? He is in bed and asleep.

GALILEO: Can't you wake him?

SIGNORA SARTI: But what do you need him for?

GALILEO: I want to show him something that will please him. I want him to see something that nobody besides ourselves has seen since the world began.

SIGNORA SARTI: Something through your tube again?

GALILEO: Something through my tube, Signora Sarti.

SIGNORA SARTI: And for that you expect me to wake him up in the middle of the night? Are you in your senses? He needs his sleep. I wouldn't think of waking him.

GALILEO: Definitely not?

SIGNORA SARTI: Definitely not.

GALILEO: Signora Sarti, perhaps you can help me then. – Look, a question has arisen about which we cannot agree, probably because we have read too many books. It is a question about the Heavens, a question concerning the stars. It is: would you say the larger revolves round the smaller, or the smaller round the larger?

SIGNORA SARTI *suspiciously*: One never know where one is with you, Signor Galilei. Is that a serious question, or are you trying to make fun of me again?

GALILEO: A serious question.

SIGNORA SARTI: Then you can have a quick answer. Do I set the dinner before you or do you set it before me?

GALILEO: You set it before me. Yesterday it was burnt.

SIGNORA SARTI: And why was it burnt? Because I had to bring you your shoes in the middle of cooking. Didn't I bring you your shoes?

GALILEO: I expect so.

SIGNORA SARTI: You see, you are the one who has studied and can pay.

GALILEO: I see. I see. That's simple. – Thank you, Signora Sarti.

Exit Signora Sarti, amused.

GALILEO: And such people cannot understand the truth? They hunger for it!

A bell for early Mass has begun to ring. Enter Virginia in a cloak carrying a shaded candle.

VIRGINIA: Good morning, father.

GALILEO: Why are you up already?

VIRGINIA: I am going with Signora Sarti to early Mass. Ludovico is coming too. What was the night like, father?

GALILEO: Clear.

VIRGINIA: May I look through it?

GALILEO: Why? *Virginia does not know what to answer.* It's not a toy.

VIRGINIA: No, father.

GALILEO: Besides, the telescope is a disappointment – you'll soon hear that everywhere. It's being sold for three scudi on the streets and has already been discovered in Holland.

VIRGINIA: Haven't you seen any more new things in the sky with it?

GALILEO: Nothing for you. Only a few small cloudy spots on the left side of a big star; somehow I shall have to draw attention to them. *Speaking across his daughter to Sagredo*: Perhaps I will christen them the 'Medicean Stars' after the Grand Duke of Florence. *To Virginia again*: You will be interested to hear, Virginia, that we shall probably be moving to Florence. I have written a letter there, asking if the Grand Duke could make use of me as Court Mathematician.

VIRGINIA *radiant*: At the Court?

SAGREDO: Galileo!

GALILEO: My friend, I need leisure. I need proofs. And I want the flesh-pots. And with that appointment I shouldn't have to drum the Ptolemaic System into the heads of private pupils. I'd have time, time, time, time, to work out my proofs – for what I have now is not enough. It's nothing, paltry jottings. With them I can't confront the whole world. As yet there is not a single proof that any celestial body revolves round the sun. But I will produce proofs, proofs for everyone from Signora Sarti up to the Pope. My one anxiety is that the Court won't take me.

VIRGINIA: Of course they will take you, father, with those new stars and everything.

GALILEO: Go to your Mass.

Exit Virginia.

GALILEO: I rarely write letters to great personages. *He hands Sagredo a letter.* Do you think I've done it all right?

SAGREDO *reads out loud the end of the letter which Galileo has given him*: 'But I desire nothing so much as to be nearer you, the rising sun that will illuminate this epoch in the world's history.' –The Grand Duke of Florence is nine.

GALILEO: That's it. I see you find my letter too servile. I have been wondering whether it is servile enough, not too formal, as if I really lacked the proper humility. A reticent letter can be written by anyone who has had the merit of expounding Aristotle, but not by me. A man such as I can only obtain a moderately dignified situation by coming crawling on his belly. And you know, I despise people whose brains are not capable of filling their bellies.

Signora Sarti and Virginia pass through on their way to Mass.

SAGREDO: Don't go to Florence, Galileo.

GALILEO: Why not?

SAGREDO: Because the monks are in control there.

GALILEO: At the Florentine court there are scholars of repute.

SAGREDO: Lackeys.

GALILEO: I will seize them by their necks and drag them in front of the telescope. Even monks are human, Sagredo. They succumb to the temptation of proof. Copernicus, don't forget, demanded that they believe his figures; but I only demand that they believe their eyes. If the truth is too weak to defend itself, it must go over to the attack. I will take hold of them and force them to look through that telescope.

SAGREDO: Galileo, I see you setting out on a fearful road. It is a night of disaster when a man sees the truth. And an hour of delusion when he believes in the commonsense of the human race. Of whom does one say 'he's going into it with his eyes open'? Of the man on the path to perdition. How could those in power leave at large a man who knows the truth, even though it be about the most distant stars? Do you think the Pope will hearken to your truth when you say he is in error, and yet not hear that he is in error? Do you think that *he* will simply write in his diary: January the tenth, 1610 – Heaven abolished? How can you wish to leave the Republic, with the truth in your pocket, and fall into the snares of monks and princes, telescope in hand? Sceptical as you are in your science, you are as credulous as a child about everything that seems to you to facilitate your tasks. You don't believe in Aristotle, but you believe in the Grand Duke of Florence. A little while ago, when I watched you at your telescope and you saw those new stars, it seemed to me as if I saw you standing amid the blazing faggots, and when you said you believed in proof, I smelt flesh burning. I love science, but I love you more, my friend. Do not go to Florence, Galileo.

GALILEO: If they accept me, I will go.

In front of the curtain appears the last page of his letter:

> When I bestow on these new stars which I have discovered the illustrious name of the Medici family, I am conscious that elevation into the starry firmament was once sufficient ennoblement for the gods and heroes, but this case is the very reverse, for the illustrious name of the Medicis will guarantee these stars immortal fame. I, however, venture to bring myself to your notice as one among the number of your most humble and devoted servants and as one who counts it his highest honour to have been born your subject.
>
> But I desire nothing so much as to be nearer to you, the rising sun that will illuminate this epoch in the world's history.
>
> Galileo Galilei

4

GALILEO HAS EXCHANGED THE REPUBLIC OF VENICE FOR THE FLORENTINE COURT. HIS DISCOVERIES WITH THE TELESCOPE MEET WITH DISBELIEF AMONG THE SAVANTS THERE.

> The Old says: As I am now, I have always been so.
> The New says: If you're no good, then go.

Galileo's House in Florence

Signora Sarti in Galileo's study, preparing it for the reception of guests. Her son, Andrea, is sitting and tidying up star-charts.

SIGNORA SARTI: Ever since we arrived in this blessed Florence, the bowing and scraping and lick-spittling has never stopped. The whole city traipses through to look at that tube, and I have to clean up the floor after them! And it's not a bit of good! If there was anything in these discoveries, the holy fathers would be the first to know. I was four years in service with Monsignor Filippo and was never able to dust all through his library. Leather books right to the ceiling and not so

much as a love poem. And the good Monsignor had a mass of
bunions on his bottom from all that sitting over his learning,
and wouldn't a man like that know what was what? And the
great viewing today will be such a fiasco that again tomorrow
I shan't be able to look the milkman in the face. I knew what
I was talking about when I advised him first to set a good
supper for the gentlemen, a nice piece of lamb, before they
look over his tube. But no! *She mimics Galileo*: 'I have something else for them.'

A sound of knocking below.

SIGNORA SARTI *looks into the spy-mirror at the window*: Heaven
save us, here's the Grand Duke already. And Galileo is still
at the University! *She runs down the stairs and lets in the Grand
Duke of Tuscany, Cosimo de' Medici, who is accompanied by his
Chamberlain and two court ladies.*

COSIMO: I want to see the telescope.

THE CHAMBERLAIN: Perhaps your Highness will wait patiently
until Signor Galilei and the other gentlemen have arrived
from the University. *To Signora Sarti*: Signor Galilei wished
the astronomers to test his discovery of the new Medicean
Stars.

COSIMO: They don't believe in the telescope. They don't at all.
And where is it?

SIGNORA SARTI: Upstairs, in his study.

*The boy nods, points up the stairs, and at a nod from Signora Sarti
runs up.*

THE CHAMBERLAIN *a very old man*: Your Highness! *To Signora
Sarti*: *Must* one go up there? I have only come because the
tutor is ill.

SIGNORA SARTI: The young gentleman will come to no harm.
My own boy is up there.

COSIMO *entering upstairs*: Good evening.

*The boys bow ceremoniously to one another. Pause. Then Andrea
turns again to his work.*

ANDREA *very like his teacher*: It's like a cross-roads here.

COSIMO: Many visitors?

ANDREA: Clumping around, gaping – and not understanding a sausage.

COSIMO: I see. Is that . . .? *He points to the telescope.*

ANDREA: Yes, that's it. But orders are: hands off!

COSIMO: And what's that? *He points at the wooden model of the Ptolemaic system.*

ANDREA: That's the Ptolemaic.

COSIMO: That shows how the sun revolves, doesn't it?

ANDREA: Yes, so they say.

COSIMO *sits down on a chair and takes the model on his lap*: My tutor's got a cold. So I was able to get away early. It's nice here.

ANDREA *restless, wanders about undecidedly, looking at the strange boy mistrustfully. At last, unable to resist the temptation any longer, he pulls out a second wooden model from behind the charts. It is a representation of the Copernican system*: But it's really like this, of course.

COSIMO: What's like that?

ANDREA *pointing to Cosimo's model*: That's what they think it's like, and this – *pointing to his model* – is what it is. The earth turns round the sun, do you see?

COSIMO: Do you really think so?

ANDREA: Of course. It's proved.

COSIMO: Really? I'd like to know why they don't ever let me see the old man any more. Yesterday he was there at supper.

ANDREA: They don't seem to believe it, eh?

COSIMO: Of course they do.

ANDREA *suddenly pointing at the model in Cosimo's lap*: Give it here. You don't even understand *that* one.

COSIMO: You don't need two.

ANDREA: Give it here. It's not a toy for little boys.

COSIMO: I don't mind giving it to you, but you must be a little more polite, you know.

ANDREA: You're a silly fool, and be polite yourself! Give it to me or you'll be sorry.

COSIMO: Don't touch me, do you hear!

They begin to struggle and are soon rolling on the floor.

ANDREA: I'll teach you how to treat a model. Give up!

COSIMO: Now it's broken. You're twisting my arm.

ANDREA: We'll soon see who's right and who's wrong. Say it revolves or I'll give you a clout on the head.

COSIMO: Never. Ow! You carrots! I'll teach you manners.

ANDREA: Carrots? Me a carrots?

They fight on in silence.
Down below Galileo and several professors of the University enter.
Behind them Federzoni.

THE CHAMBERLAIN: Gentlemen, a slight indisposition has prevented His Highness's tutor, Signor Suri, from accompanying His Highness here.

THE THEOLOGIAN: Nothing serious, I trust?

THE CHAMBERLAIN: Not at all. Not at all.

GALILEO *disappointed*: His Highness is not here?

THE CHAMBERLAIN: His Highness is upstairs. But pray, gentlemen, do not wait. The Court is exceedingly curious to learn the illustrious University's opinion on this extraordinary instrument of Signor Galilei's and to become acquainted with his wonderful new stars.

They go up.
The boys are lying still, having heard the sounds downstairs.

COSIMO: They're here. Let me up.

They get up quickly.

VARIOUS GENTLEMEN *as they climb the stairs*: No, no, everything's perfectly all right. – The medical faculty declare it impossible for the sickness in the Old Town to be cases of plague. The miasmas would freeze at the present temperature. – The worst thing in such circumstances is always panic. – Nothing but the epidemic of colds usual at this time of year. – Any suspicion out of the question. – Everything's perfectly all right.

Greetings upstairs.

D

GALILEO: Your Highness, I am happy, in your presence, to be able to acquaint the gentlemen of your University with my latest discoveries.

Cosimo bows very formally in all directions, even to Andrea.

THE THEOLOGIAN *seeing the broken Ptolemaic model on the floor*: Something seems to have got broken here.

Cosimo bends down quickly and politely hands the model to Andrea. Meanwhile Galileo surreptitiously moves the other model out of sight.

GALILEO *at the telescope*: As your Highness doubtless knows, for some time past we astronomers have been in great difficulties with our calculations. For these we use a very old system which appears to coincide with philosophy, but not, alas, with facts. According to this old system – the Ptolemaic – the movements of the stars are presumed to be extremely complicated. For instance, the planet Venus is supposed to follow an orbit of this sort. *On the blackboard he draws the epicyclic orbit of Venus according to the Ptolemaic conception.* But even accepting such complicated movements, we are still not able to calculate the positions of the stars correctly. We do not find them in the places where they apparently should be. And furthermore there are certain movements of the stars for which the Ptolemaic system has no explanation at all. Movements of this sort seem to me to be described by the little stars round the planet Jupiter, which I have recently discovered. Would the gentlemen care to begin with an observation of the satellites of Jupiter, the Medicean stars?

ANDREA *pointing to the stool in front of the telescope*: Please sit here.

THE PHILOSOPHER: Thank you, my child. I fear that things are not quite as simple as all that. Signor Galilei, before we apply ourselves to your famous instrument we would like to have the pleasure of a disputation. The theme: Can such planets exist?

THE MATHEMATICIAN: A formal disputation.

GALILEO: I thought you could simply look through the telescope and convince yourselves.

ANDREA: Here, please.

THE MATHEMATICIAN: Of course, of course. – Naturally, you know that according to the ancient stars revolving about a centre other than the earth cannot exist, nor can there be stars which have no support in the Heavens?

GALILEO: Yes.

THE PHILOSOPHER: And quite apart from the possibility of such stars, which the mathematician – *he bows to the mathematician* – appears to doubt, I would, in all modesty, as a philosopher, like to pose the question: are such stars necessary? Aristotelis divini universum . . .

GALILEO: Should we not continue in the vernacular? My colleague, Signor Federzoni, does not understand Latin.

THE PHILOSOPHER: Is it of importance that he should understand us?

GALILEO: Yes.

THE PHILOSOPHER: Excuse me. I thought he was your lens-grinder.

ANDREA: Signor Federzoni is a lens-grinder and a scholar.

THE PHILOSOPHER: Thank you, my child. If Signor Federzoni insists . . .

GALILEO: *I* insist.

THE PHILOSOPHER: The argument will lose in elegance, but it is your house. – The cosmos of the divine Aristotle, with its mystical, music-making spheres and crystal domes and the gyrations of its heavenly bodies and the oblique angle of the sun's orbit and the secrets of the satellite tables and the rich catalogue of constellations in the southern hemisphere and the inspired construction of the celestial globe, is a conception of such symmetry and beauty that we should do well to hesitate before disturbing that harmony.

GALILEO: How would it be if your Highness were now to observe these impossible as well as unnecessary stars through this telescope?

THE MATHEMATICIAN: One might be tempted to reply that your

telescope, showing something which cannot exist, may not be a very reliable telescope, eh?

GALILEO: What do you mean?

THE MATHEMATICIAN: It would be much more helpful, Signor Galilei, if you were to tell us the reasons which lead you to the assumption that in the highest spheres of the immutable Heavens stars can move freely through space.

THE PHILOSOPHER: Reasons, Signor Galilei, reasons.

GALILEO: The reasons? – When a glance at the stars themselves and my own observations will demonstrate the phenomenon. Sir, the disputation is becoming absurd.

THE MATHEMATICIAN: If one could be sure that you would not excite yourself further, one might suggest that what is in your telescope and what is in the Heavens may be two different things.

THE PHILOSOPHER: That could not have been more courteously expressed.

FEDERZONI: You think we painted the Medicean stars on the lens!

GALILEO: Are you accusing me of fraud?

THE PHILOSOPHER: But how could we? In the presence of his Highness!

THE MATHEMATICIAN: Your instrument – whether one calls it your child or your pupil – is certainly most cleverly made, no doubt about that!

THE PHILOSOPHER: And we are entirely convinced, Signor Galilei, that neither you nor anyone else would dare to bestow the illustrious name of our ruling house on stars whose existence was not beyond all possible doubt.

They all bow low to the Grand Duke.

COSIMO *looks round to the court ladies*: Is there something not right with my stars?

THE OLDER COURT LADY *to the Grand Duke*: Everything is all right with the stars, your Highness. The gentlemen are only asking whether they really and truly are there.

Pause.

THE YOUNGER COURT LADY: One is said to be able to see every hair on the Great Bear through that instrument.

FEDERZONI: Yes, and all sorts of things on the Bull.

GALILEO: Well, will you gentlemen now look through it, or not?

THE PHILOSOPHER: Certainly, of course.

THE MATHEMATICIAN: Of course.

Pause. Suddenly Andrea turns and walks stiffly across the whole room. His mother catches hold of him.

SIGNORA SARTI: What's the matter with you?

ANDREA: They're stupid. *He tears himself loose and runs off.*

THE PHILOSOPHER: Deplorable child.

THE CHAMBERLAIN: Your Highness, gentlemen, may I remind you that the Court Ball opens in three-quarters of an hour?

THE MATHEMATICIAN: Why mince matters? Sooner or later Signor Galilei will have to reconcile himself with the facts. His planets of Jupiter would break through the crystal spheres. It is quite simple.

FEDERZONI: You'll be astonished! There are no crystal spheres.

THE PHILOSOPHER: Every school-book will tell you they exist, my good man.

FEDERZONI: Then hurrah for new school-books.

THE PHILOSOPHER: Your Highness, my worthy colleague and I rely on the authority of none less than the divine Aristotle himself.

GALILEO *almost obsequiously*: Gentlemen, belief in the authority of Aristotle is one thing; facts, tangible facts, are another. You say that according to Aristotle there are crystal spheres up there and therefore certain movements cannot take place because the stars would have to break through those spheres. But what if you can confirm those movements? Perhaps that will persuade you that those crystal spheres simply don't exist. Gentlemen, I beseech you in all humility to trust your eyes.

THE MATHEMATICIAN: My dear Galileo, old-fashioned though it may sound to you, I am accustomed among other things to

read Aristotle, and I can assure you that there I do trust my
eyes.

GALILEO: I am used to seeing members of all faculties shutting
their eyes against every fact and behaving as though nothing
has happened. I offer my observations, and they smile. I place
my telescope at their disposal so that they can convince themselves, and they quote Aristotle. But the man had no telescope!

THE MATHEMATICIAN: Certainly not. Certainly not.

THE PHILOSOPHER *sweepingly*: If Aristotle – an authority recognised not only by the entire learning of antiquity but also by
the Holy Fathers of the Church – if Aristotle is to be dragged
through the mud, then it seems, to me at least, that a con-
tinuation of this discussion is superfluous. I avoid pointless
discussion. Enough!

GALILEO: Truth is the child of time, not of authority. Our ignor-
ance is infinite, so let us diminish it by a fraction. Why try to
be so clever now, when at last we can become a little less
stupid? I have had the unbelievable good fortune to lay my
hands on a new instrument by means of which one can see
one tiny corner of the universe a little clearer. Not much –
but a little. Make use of it!

THE PHILOSOPHER: Your Highness, ladies and gentlemen, I am
just asking myself where all this may lead.

GALILEO: I would suggest that as scientists it is not for us to ask
where the truth may lead us.

THE PHILOSOPHER *furiously*: Signor Galilei, the truth may lead
us to absolutely anything.

GALILEO: Your Highness. On nights such as these, all over Italy
telescopes are being turned towards the Heavens. Jupiter's
moons will not make milk any cheaper. But they have never
been seen before, and they are there. From that the man in
the street draws the conclusion that there may be many more
things to see if only he opens his eyes. You owe him that
confirmation. It is not the movements of a few distant stars
that make all Italy prick up its ears, but the news that opinions
hitherto held inviolable have now begun to totter – and

everyone knows there are too many of those. Gentlemen, let us not defend dying teachings.

FEDERZONI: You, as teachers, should hasten their end.

THE PHILOSOPHER: I should prefer your man not to proffer advice in a scientific disputation.

GALILEO: Your Highness. My work in the Great Arsenal of Venice brought me into daily contact with draughtsmen, builders and instrument-makers. These people taught me many a new way of doing things. Illiterate, they relied on the evidence of their five senses, in most cases regardless of where such evidence might lead them . . .

THE PHILOSOPHER: Oho!

GALILEO: Very like our mariners, who a hundred years ago left our shores without knowing what sort of other shores they might reach, if any at all. It seems that today, in order to find that high curiosity which made the true greatness of ancient Greece, one has to resort to the shipyards.

THE PHILOSOPHER: After all that we have heard here, I have no longer any doubt that Signor Galilei will find admirers in the shipyards.

THE CHAMBERLAIN: Your Highness, to my dismay I find that this extraordinarily instructive conversation has become somewhat long drawn out. Your Highness must rest a while before the Court Ball.

At a sign the Grand Duke bows to Galileo. The Court rapidly begins to leave.

SIGNORA SARTI *places herself in front of the Grand Duke and offers him a plate of pastries*: A biscuit, your Highness?

The older court lady leads the Grand Duke out.

GALILEO *running after them*: But really, you gentlemen need only look through the instrument!

THE CHAMBERLAIN: His Highness will not fail to obtain an opinion on your claims from the greatest living astronomer, Father Christopher Clavius, Astronomer-in-Chief at the Papal College in Rome.

5

UNDAUNTED EVEN BY THE PLAGUE, GALILEO CONTINUES HIS RESEARCHES

a

Galileo's Study in Florence

Early morning. Galileo over his notes, at the telescope. Enter Virginia with a travelling bag.

GALILEO: Virginia! Has something happened?

VIRGINIA: The convent has closed; we have been sent straight home. There are five cases of plague in Arcetri.

GALILEO *calls out*: Sarti!

VIRGINIA: The market-street has been closed off since this morning. In the Old Town there are said to be two dead and three dying in hospital.

GALILEO: Once again they've kept everything secret till the last moment.

SIGNORA SARTI *enters*: What are you doing here?

VIRGINIA: The plague.

SIGNORA SARTI: My God! I'll pack. *She sits down.*

GALILEO: Pack nothing. Take Virginia and Andrea. I'll collect my notes.

He runs quickly back to his table and shovels papers together in great haste. Signora Sarti puts a cloak on to Andrea, who has come running in, and fetches some bedding and food. Enter a grand-ducal lackey.

LACKEY: His Highness, on account of the prevailing sickness, has left the city for Bologna. But he insists that Signor Galilei be offered the opportunity of being brought to safety as well. The carriage will be at the door in two minutes.

SIGNORA SARTI *to Virginia and Andrea*: Go, go quickly. Here, take that with you.

ANDREA: But why? If you don't tell me why, I shan't go.

SIGNORA SARTI: It's the plague, my child.

VIRGINIA: We will wait for father.

SIGNORA SARTI: Signor Galilei, are you ready?

GALILEO *who is wrapping the telescope in the table-cloth*: Put Virginia and Andrea in the carriage. I'll come immediately.

VIRGINIA: No. We won't go without you. You'll never be ready if you once start packing your books.

SIGNORA SARTI: The coach is here.

GALILEO: Be sensible, Virginia; if you two don't get in, the coachman will drive away. The plague – that's no light matter.

VIRGINIA *protesting, as Signora Sarti shepherds her and Andrea out*: Help him with his books, otherwise he'll never come.

SIGNORA SARTI *calls from the front door*: Signor Galilei, the coachman refuses to wait!

GALILEO: Signora Sarti, I do not think I should leave. Everything is in disorder, you know; I might as well throw away the last three months' notes if I cannot go on with them for one or two more nights. And this pestilence is everywhere, after all.

SIGNORA SARTI: Signor Galilei! Come down at once. You are out of your mind!

GALILEO: You must go on with Virginia and Andrea. I'll follow later.

SIGNORA SARTI: In another hour no one will be allowed to leave the city. You must come! *She listens.* He is driving off! I must stop him!

Exit.

Galileo walks backwards and forwards. Signora Sarti returns, very pale, without her bundle of luggage.

GALILEO: Why are you standing about? The carriage with the children will go off without you.

SIGNORA SARTI: They have gone. They had to hold Virginia in. Someone will look after the children in Bologna. But who would prepare your food here?

GALILEO: You are out of your mind. To **stay** in the city for the sake of cooking . . .! *He picks up his notes.* Don't think I am a fool, Signora Sarti. I cannot abandon my observations. I have powerful enemies and must collect my proofs for certain theories.

SIGNORA SARTI: You don't need to apologise. But it's not sensible.

b

Outside Galileo's House in Florence

Galileo steps out and looks down the street. Two nuns walk past.

GALILEO *addresses them*: Can you tell me, sisters, where I can buy some milk? This morning the milk-woman did not come and my housekeeper is out.

A NUN: Shops are open only in the Lower Town now.

ANOTHER NUN: Have you come out of there? *Galileo nods.* This is the street!

Both nuns cross themselves, murmur a Hail Mary and hurry away. A man comes along.

GALILEO *addresses him*: Aren't you the baker who brings us white bread? *The man nods.* Have you seen my housekeeper? She must have gone out yesterday evening. She wasn't in the house this morning.

The man shakes his head.
A window opposite opens and a woman looks out.

THE WOMAN *shouting*: Run! They have the plague over there!

The man runs away in terror.

GALILEO: Do you know anything about my housekeeper?

THE WOMAN: Your housekeeper collapsed down the street. She must have known it. That's why she left. Such inconsiderateness! *She slams the window shut.*

Some children come down the street. They see Galileo and run away screaming. Galileo turns and two soldiers covered from head to foot in armour come running in.

SOLDIERS: Back into your house immediately!

With their long lances they push Galileo back into his house. Behind him they barricade the door.

GALILEO *at the window*: Can you tell me what has happened to my housekeeper?

SOLDIERS: They are all being taken to the meadows.

THE WOMAN *appears at her window again*: The whole of that side of the street is plagued. Why don't you close it off?

The soldiers tie a rope across the street.

THE WOMAN: But now no one can get into our house either! There's no need to shut *us* off! Everyone is healthy here. Stop! Stop! Listen to me. My husband is still in the town, and he won't be able to get back to us. You brutes, you brutes!

She can be heard inside sobbing and screaming. The soldiers go off. At another window appears an old woman.

GALILEO: There must be a fire over there.

THE OLD WOMAN: They no longer put a fire out where plague is suspected. No one thinks of anything but plague.

GALILEO: How like them that is! That's their whole system of government. They lop us off like the infected branch of a fig-tree that can no longer bear fruit.

THE OLD WOMAN: You mustn't say that. They are just helpless.

GALILEO: Are you alone in the house?

THE OLD WOMAN: Yes. My son sent me a note. Thank God, he discovered yesterday evening that someone had died over there, and he didn't come home. There were eleven cases last night in this district.

GALILEO: I reproach myself for not having sent my housekeeper away in time. I had urgent work, but she had no reason to stay.

THE OLD WOMAN: We can't go either, now. Who would take us in? You mustn't reproach yourself. I saw her. She went out this morning early, about seven o'clock. She was ill, for when she saw me come out of the door to take in my bread, she gave me a wide berth. She probably didn't want them to close your house. But they find out everything.

There is the sound of a rattle.

GALILEO: What is that?

THE OLD WOMAN: They make those noises to try and disperse the clouds that harbour the plague seeds.

Galileo laughs loudly.

And you can laugh!

A man comes down the street and finds it barred by the rope.

GALILEO: Hi, you! I am locked in here and there is nothing to eat in the house.

The man has already run away.

GALILEO: But you can't leave us to starve here! Hi! Hi!

THE OLD WOMAN: Perhaps they will bring something. Otherwise, but only after dark, I can leave a jug of milk outside your door if you are not afraid.

GALILEO: Hi! Hi! Someone must hear us!

Andrea suddenly stands by the rope. His face is stained with tears.

GALILEO: Andrea! How did you get here?

ANDREA: I was here earlier. I knocked, but you didn't open. The people told me that . . .

GALILEO: Didn't you leave in the carriage?

ANDREA: Yes, but on the way I managed to jump off. Virginia has gone on. Can't I come in?

THE OLD WOMAN: No, that you can't. You must go to the Ursulines. Your mother may be there.

ANDREA: I've been there. But they wouldn't let me see her. She is so ill.

GALILEO: Have you walked all the way here? It is three days since you left.

ANDREA: It took me that long; don't be angry with me. They caught me once.

GALILEO *helplessly*: Stop crying now. Look, I have discovered all sorts of things in the meanwhile. Shall I tell you? *Andrea nods, sobbing.* Well, listen carefully or you won't understand. Do you remember when I showed you the planet Venus? Don't listen to that noise, that's nothing. Can you remember?

Do you know what I have seen? It is like the moon! I have seen it as a hemisphere and I have seen it as a crescent. What do you say to that? I can show it all to you with a little ball and a candle. It proves that that planet, too, has no light of its own. And it revolves round the sun, in a simple circle. Isn't that wonderful?

ANDREA *sobbing*: Yes, and it's a fact.

GALILEO *softly*: I didn't keep her here.

Andrea is silent.

GALILEO: But of course if I hadn't stayed, it wouldn't have happened.

ANDREA: Will they have to believe you now?

GALILEO: I have assembled all my proofs now. Do you know, when this is all over, I shall go to Rome and show them.

Down the street come two men, muffled up and carrying long poles with buckets on the end. They pass bread, first to Galileo and then to the old woman, through the windows.

THE OLD WOMAN: And over there is a woman with three children. Put in something for them, too.

GALILEO: But I have nothing to drink. There is no water in the house. *The two men shrug their shoulders.* Will you be coming again tomorrow?

ONE OF THE MEN *in a smothered voice as he has a cloth over his mouth*: Who knows today what tomorrow will bring?

GALILEO: If you do come could you also hand me a little book that I need for my work?

THE MAN *laughs hollowly*: As if a book mattered now! Be thankful if you get your bread.

GALILEO: But that boy, my pupil, will be here to give it to you for me. – It's the map with the period of rotation of Mercury, Andrea; I've mislaid it. Will you get one from the school?

The two men have already walked away.

ANDREA: Of course. I'll fetch it, Signor Galilei. *Exit.*

Galileo withdraws from the window. From the house opposite the old woman steps out and places a jug by Galileo's door.

6

1616: THE COLLEGIUM ROMANUM, THE VATICAN'S
INSTITUTE OF RESEARCH, CONFIRMS GALILEO'S DIS-
COVERIES

> Things take indeed a wondrous turn
> When learned men do stoop to learn.
> Clavius, we are pleased to say,
> Upheld Galileo Galilei

Hall of the Collegium Romanum in Rome

It is night. High church dignitaries, monks and scholars in groups. To one side stands Galileo – alone. The atmosphere is very boisterous. Before the scene begins one hears roars of thunderous laughter.

THE FAT PRELATE *clutching his stomach with mirth*: Oh stupidity! Oh stupidity! I wish someone would tell me one proposition that would *not* be believed!

THE SCHOLAR: For example, that you have an unconquerable aversion to dining, monsignor!

THE FAT PRELATE: They'd believe it! They'd believe it! Only the reasonable is not believed. That a Devil exists – that's doubted. But that the earth spins round like a marble in the gutter – that's believed! Sancta simplicitas!

A MONK *play-acting*: I feel dizzy. The earth's turning too fast. Permit me to hold on to you, professor. *He pretends to sway and clings to one of the scholars.*

THE SCHOLAR *joining in the game*: Yes, she's drunk again today, our dear old Mother Earth. *He clutches at another.*

THE MONK: Stop, stop! We're slipping off. Stop, I say!

A SECOND SCHOLAR: Venus is quite crooked already. I can only see half of her behind! Help!

A group of monks collects. Laughing, they act as if trying to save themselves from being thrown off a ship in a storm.

A SECOND MONK: If only we don't get flung on to the moon. Brothers, they say it's got horribly sharp mountain peaks!

THE FIRST SCHOLAR: Steady yourself with your feet.

THE FIRST MONK: And don't look down. I get giddy.

THE FAT PRELATE *intentionally loud, in Galileo's direction*: Impossible! Giddiness in the Collegium Romanum!

Loud laughter.
Through the door at the back enter two astronomers of the College.
Silence falls.

A MONK: Are you still investigating? Scandalous!

THE FIRST ASTRONOMER *angrily*: *We* are not!

THE SECOND ASTRONOMER: Where will this lead? I cannot understand Clavius ... If one had accepted as sterling truth everything claimed during the past five years! In the year 1572, in the highest sphere, the eighth, the sphere of fixed stars, a new constellation blazes, far brighter and larger than all its neighbours, and before eighteen months have passed it vanishes again and returns to oblivion. Might one ask: what of the eternal duration and immutability of the Heavens?

THE PHILOSOPHER: If one let them, they would demolish our whole universe.

THE FIRST ASTRONOMER: Yes, what are we coming to? Five years later the Dane, Tycho Brahe, determines the track of a comet. It started up above the moon and broke through one after another of the crystal spheres, the solid carriers of the moving constellations! It meets with no resistance, it suffers no refraction of its light. Should one ask: where are the spheres?

THE PHILOSOPHER: Quite out of the question! How can Christopher Clavius, Italy's and the Church's greatest astronomer, even investigate such a thing?

THE FAT PRELATE: Scandalous!

THE FIRST ASTRONOMER: But he *is* investigating it! He's sitting in there and peering through that devil's tube!

THE SECOND ASTRONOMER: Principiis obsta! It all began by our calculating so many things from the tables of Copernicus, who is a heretic! The length of the solar years, the dates of eclipses of the sun and moon, the positions of the celestial bodies for years ahead.

A MONK: I ask you which is better: to experience an eclipse

three days after it appears in the calendar, or eternal salvation never?

A VERY THIN MONK *steps forward with an open Bible, pointing his finger fanatically at a passage*: What is said in the Holy Writ? 'Sun, stand thou still upon Gibeon; and thou, Moon, in the Valley of Ajalon.' How can the sun stand still if it never moves, as these heretics aver? Does Holy Writ lie?

THE FIRST ASTRONOMER: No – and that is why we are leaving.

THE SECOND ASTRONOMER: There are phenomena which present difficulties to us astronomers, but does man have to understand everything?

Both exeunt.

THE VERY THIN MONK: They equate the home of the human race to a wandering star. They pack men, animals, plants, and the earth itself on to a cart and trundle it in a circle through an empty sky. Earth and Heaven exist no more according to them. The earth no more, because it is a star in Heaven; and Heaven no more, because it is made up of earths. There is no longer any difference between the Upper and the Lower. Between the Eternal and the Temporal. That we pass away, we know. That Heaven too passes away, they now inform us. There are sun, moon and stars, and we live on the earth; so it was said, and so it is written. But now the earth, too, is a star according to them. There is nothing but stars! We shall yet live to see the day when they will say: there are no longer men and animals, man is an animal, there is nothing but animals!

THE FIRST SCHOLAR *to Galileo*: Signor Galilei, you have dropped something on the floor.

GALILEO *who during the foregoing has taken his stone out of a pocket, played with it, and finally let it fall to the ground, as he stoops to pick it up*: No, Monsignor. It fell up to me.

THE FAT PRELATE *turning away*: Impudent rascal.

Enter a very old cardinal supported by a monk. Everyone respectfully makes way for him.

THE VERY OLD CARDINAL: Are they still in there? Can they really not dispose of this triviality more quickly? Clavius ought to understand his own astronomy. I hear that this Signor Galilei banishes mankind from the centre of the universe to somewhere at the edge. He is, therefore, plainly an enemy of the human race. And he should be treated as such. Man is the crown of creation, every child knows that, God's highest and most beloved creature. How could He place such a miracle, such a masterpiece, on a little remote and for ever wandering star? Would He have sent His Son to such a place? How can there be people so perverse as to believe in these slaves of their own mathematical tables? Which of God's creatures would submit to such a thing?

THE FAT PRELATE *sotto voce*: The gentleman is present.

THE VERY OLD CARDINAL *to Galileo*: So you are the person? I no longer see very well, but what I can see is enough to show me that you are remarkably like that man we burnt here in his time. What was his name?

THE MONK: Your Eminence should not excite himself. The doctor . . .

THE VERY OLD CARDINAL *shaking him off, to Galileo*: You wish to degrade the earth, although you live on it and receive everything from it. You would foul your own nest! But I at least will have none of it! *He pushes the monk away and begins proudly pacing up and down.* I am not just any being on just any little star circling round somewhere for a short time. I tread the firm earth, with a sure step; it is at rest; it is the centre of the universe; I am at the centre, and the eye of the Creator rests on me and on me alone. Around me revolve, attached to eight crystalline spheres, the fixed stars and the mighty sun which was created to shed light upon my surroundings. And upon me too, in order that God may see me. And so, visibly and irrefutably, everything depends on me, on Man, the masterpiece of God, the centre of Creation, the very image of God, immortal and . . . *He collapses.*

THE MONK: Your Eminence has overstrained himself.

At this moment the door at the back opens and the great Clavius enters at the head of his astronomers. He walks through the hall hurriedly and in silence, not looking to right or left. Just as he is leaving the hall he speaks to a monk.

CLAVIUS: He is right.

He goes out, followed by the astronomers. The door at the back remains open. A dead silence falls. The very old cardinal revives.

THE VERY OLD CARDINAL: What is it? Have they reached a decision?

No one dares to tell him.

THE MONK: Your Eminence must be taken home.

The old man is helped out. All leave the hall bewildered. A little monk from Clavius' commission of investigation stops beside Galileo.

THE LITTLE MONK *surreptitiously*: Signor Galilei, Father Clavius said before he left: Now let the theologians see how they can put their heavenly rings together again! You have won. *Exit.*

GALILEO *tries to hold him back*: It has won! Not I but commonsense has won!

The little monk has already gone. Galileo leaves too. In the doorway he encounters a tall priest, the Cardinal Inquisitor. An astronomer accompanies him. Galileo bows. Before he goes out, he whispers a question to the lackey at the door.

THE LACKEY *whispering back*: His Eminence, the Cardinal Inquisitor. *The astronomer leads the Cardinal Inquisitor to the Telescope.*

7

BUT THE INQUISITION PUTS THE COPERNICAN TEACHINGS ON THE INDEX (MARCH 5TH, 1616)

> When Galileo was in Rome
> A Cardinal asked him to his home
> He wined and dined him as his guest
> And only made one small request.

Cardinal Bellarmin's House in Rome

A ball is in progress. In the vestibule, where two clerks in holy orders are playing chess and making notes about the guests, Galileo is received with applause by a little group of masked ladies and gentlemen. He arrives in the company of his daughter, Virginia, and her betrothed, Ludovico Marsili.

VIRGINIA: I shall dance with no one else, Ludovico.

LUDOVICO: Your shoulder-strap is loose.

GALILEO:

> 'Fret not, daughter, if perchance
> You attract a wanton glance.
> The eyes that catch a trembling lace
> Will guess the heartbeat's quickened pace.
> Lovely women still may be
> Careless with felicity.'

VIRGINIA: Feel my heart.

GALILEO *lays his hand on her heart*: It's beating.

VIRGINIA: I want to look beautiful.

GALILEO: You must, or people will soon start wondering once more whether the earth really goes round.

LUDOVICO: But it doesn't. *Galileo laughs.* All Rome talks of nothing but you. But after this evening, Signor, it's your daughter they'll be talking about.

GALILEO: They say it is easy to look beautiful in the Roman springtime. Even I must resemble a slightly corpulent Adonis. *To the two young clerks.* I am supposed to await the Cardinal here. *To the young couple.* Go and enjoy yourselves.

Before they go off to join the ball, Virginia comes running back once more.

VIRGINIA: Father, the hairdresser in the Via del Trionfo took me first and let four other ladies wait. He knew your name immediately. *Exit.*

GALILEO *to the clerks playing chess*: How can you still play that old-fashioned chess? Narrow, narrow. Nowadays people play with the important pieces moving all over the board. The rook like that – *he demonstrates* – and the bishop like that, and the queen here and here. That gives room, and you can lay your plans.

A CLERK: That is not commensurate with our small salaries, you know. We can only afford moves like this. *He makes a tiny move.*

GALILEO: On the contrary, my friend, on the contrary. Who takes big steps is given big boots. One must move with the times, gentlemen. No hugging the coast; sometimes you must put out to sea.

The very old Cardinal from the previous scene crosses the stage, accompanied by his monk. He catches sight of Galileo, walks past him, then turns uncertainly and greets him. Galileo sits down. From the ballroom can be heard boys' voices singing the beginning of Lorenzo de' Medici's famous poem on fugacity:

> 'I, who have seen the summer's roses die
> And all their petals pale and shrivelled lie
> Upon the chilly ground, I know the truth:
> How evanescent is the flower of youth.'

GALILEO: Rome. – Great celebrations?

FIRST CLERK: The first carnival since the plague years. All the great families in Italy are represented here this evening. The Orsinis, the Villanis, the Nuccolis, the Soldanieris, the Canes, the Lecchis, the Estes, the Colombinis . . .

SECOND CLERK *interrupts*: Their Eminences the Cardinals Bellarmin and Barberini.

Enter Cardinal Bellarmin and Cardinal Barberini. In front of their faces they each hold a mask of a lamb and a dove respectively on the end of a stick.

BARBERINI *pointing his index finger at Galileo*: 'The sun also ariseth, and the sun goeth down, and hasteneth to his place where he arose.' So saith Ecclesiastes, the Preacher. And what says Galileo?

GALILEO: When I was so high, your Eminence – *he indicates with his hand* – I stood on a ship and I cried out: the shore is moving away! Today I know that the shore stood still and the ship moved away.

BARBERINI: Shrewd, shrewd. What one sees, Bellarmin, namely the constellations revolving, need not be true; think of the ship and the shore. But what is true, namely that the earth rotates, cannot be seen! Shrewd. But his moons of Jupiter are hard nuts for our astronomers to crack. Unfortunately, I too read some astronomy at one time, Bellarmin. It sticks to one like a burr.

BELLARMIN: Let us move with the times, Barberini. If star-charts based on a new hypothesis simplify navigation for our sailors, then let them use these charts. We only dislike teachings which contradict the Bible. *He waves in greeting towards the ballroom.*

GALILEO: The Bible. – 'He that withholdeth corn, the people shall curse him.' Proverbs.

BARBERINI: 'Wise men lay up knowledge.' Proverbs.

GALILEO: 'Where no oxen are, the crib is clean; but much increase is by the strength of the ox.'

BARBERINI: 'He that ruleth his spirit is better than he that taketh a city.'

GALILEO: 'But a broken spirit drieth the house.' *Pause.* 'Doth not truth cry aloud?'

BARBERINI: 'Can one go upon hot coals and his feet not be burned?' Welcome in Rome, friend Galileo. You know her origin? Two little boys, so runs the legend, received milk and shelter from a she-wolf. From that hour on, all children have had to pay for the she-wolf's milk. But in return the she-wolf provides all sorts of pleasures, heavenly and earthly, ranging from conversations with my learned friend Bellarmin to the company of three or four ladies of international reputation. May I display them to you?

He leads Galileo to the rear, in order to show him the ballroom. Galileo follows reluctantly.

BARBERINI: No? He insists on a serious conversation. All right. Are you sure, friend Galileo, that you astronomers are not simply concerned with making your astronomy more manageable? *He leads him to the front again.* You think in terms of circles and ellipses and equal velocities, simple movements that your mind can grasp. But what if it had pleased God to make his stars move like this? *With his finger moving at varying speeds he describes in the air an extremely complicated track.*

GALILEO: Your Eminence, if God had constructed the universe like that – *he repeats Barberini's track* – then he would also have constructed our grains like that – *he repeats the same track* – so that they would recognise these very tracks as the simplest possible. I believe in reason.

BARBERINI: I hold reason to be inadequate. – He is silent. He is too polite to say now that he holds me to be inadequate. *He laughs and returns to the balustrade at the back.*

BELLARMIN: Reason, my friend, does not reach very far. All around we see nothing but crookedness, crime and weakness. Where is truth?

GALILEO *angrily*: I believe in reason.

BARBERINI *to the clerks*: There is no need to take this down. This is a scientific conversation between friends.

BELLARMIN: Consider for a moment all the trouble and thought it cost the Fathers of the Church, and so many after them, to bring a little sense into this world (is it not a little repellent?). Consider the brutality of the landlords in the Campagna who have their peasants whipped half-naked over their estates, and the stupidity of those poor people who kiss their feet in return.

GALILEO: Horrible! On my journey here I saw . . .

BELLARMIN: We have placed the responsibility for the meaning of such happenings as we cannot comprehend – life consists of them – on a higher Being, and we have explained that such things are the result of certain intentions, that all this happens according to one great plan. Not that this has brought about complete reassurance; but now you have to accuse this supreme Being of not knowing for certain how the stars move, a matter on which *you* are perfectly clear. Is that wise?

GALILEO *preparing to explain*: I am a true son of the Church . . .

BARBERINI: He is incorrigible. In all innocence he tries to prove God a complete fool on the subject of astronomy! Do you mean that God did not study astronomy sufficiently before he indited the Holy Scriptures? My dear friend!

BELLARMIN: Does it not appear probable to you that the Creator knows more about His own handiwork than does the handiwork itself?

GALILEO: But, gentlemen, man can misinterpret not only the movements of the stars, but the Bible too.

BELLARMIN: But the interpretation of the Bible is, after all, the business of the theologians of the Holy Church, eh?

Galileo is silent.

BELLARMIN: You see. You are silent now. *He makes a sign to the clerks.* Signor Galilei, tonight the Holy Office has decided that the teachings of Copernicus, according to which the sun is the centre of the universe and motionless, while the earth is not the centre of the universe and is moving, are futile, foolish and heretical. I have been entrusted with the duty of informing you of this decision. *To the first clerk*: Repeat that.

FIRST CLERK: His Eminence Cardinal Bellarmin to the aforementioned Galileo Galilei: The Holy Office has decided that the teachings of Copernicus, according to which the sun is the centre of the universe and motionless, while the earth is not the centre of the universe and is moving, are futile, foolish and heretical. I have been entrusted with the duty of informing you of this decision.

GALILEO: What does that mean?

From the ballroom can be heard boys' voices singing another verse of the poem:

> 'I said: the lovely season flieth fast;
> So pluck the rose – it still is May.'

Barberini gestures Galileo to be silent while the song lasts. They listen.

GALILEO: But the facts? I understood that the astronomers of the Collegium Romanum had accepted my observations.

BELLARMIN: With the expression of the deepest satisfaction, which does you the greatest honour.

GALILEO: But the satellites of Jupiter, the phases of Venus . . .

BELLARMIN: The Holy Congregation has made its decision without considering these details.

GALILEO: That means that all further scientific research . . .

BELLARMIN: Is well assured, Signor Galilei. And that, in conformity with the Church's view that we cannot know, but we may research. *He again greets a guest in the ballroom.* You are at liberty to expound even this teaching through mathematical hypotheses. Science is the legitimate and dearly beloved daughter of the Church, Signor Galilei. Not one of us seriously believes that you desire to undermine the authority of the Church.

GALILEO *angrily*: Authority grows feeble from being abused.

BARBERINI: Does it? *He claps him on the shoulder, laughing loudly. Then he looks sharply at him and says, not unkindly*: Don't throw out the baby with the bath-water, friend Galileo. We don't do that either. We need you, more than you need us.

BELLARMIN: I am burning to present the greatest mathematician in Italy to the President of the Holy Office, who regards you with the utmost admiration.

BARBERINI *catching hold of Galileo's other arm*: Whereupon he is once more transformed into a lamb. You too, my dear friend, would have done better to appear here costumed as the worthy doctor of school tradition. It is my mask that permits me a little freedom today. In such a get-up you might hear me murmuring: if there were no God, one would have to

invent one. Good, let us put up our masks again. Poor Galilei
has none. *They take Galileo between them and lead him into the
ballroom.*

FIRST CLERK: Did you get the last sentence?

SECOND CLERK: I did. *They write industriously.* Have you got down
the bit where he says that he believes in reason?

Enter the Cardinal Inquisitor.

THE INQUISITOR: Did the conversation take place?

FIRST CLERK *mechanically*: At first Signor Galilei came in with
his daughter. Today she became engaged to Signor . . . *The
Inquisitor stops him impatiently.* Signor Galilei then instructed
us in the new manner of playing chess in which the pieces
move all over the board contrary to the rules of the game.

THE INQUISITOR *gestures him to silence*: The transcript.

*A clerk hands it to him, and he sits down to glance through it. Two
young ladies, masked, cross the stage. They curtsey in front of the
cardinal.*

ONE YOUNG LADY: Who is that?

THE OTHER: The Cardinal Inquisitor.

*They giggle and go off. Enter Virginia, looking round in search of
something.*

THE INQUISITOR *from his corner*: Well, my daughter?

VIRGINIA *starts, for she has not seen him*: Oh, your Eminence!

*Without looking up, the Inquisitor stretches out his right hand. She
approaches, kneels and kisses his ring.*

THE INQUISITOR: A superb night! Permit me to congratulate you
on your engagement. Your bridegroom comes from a noble
family. You will remain with us in Rome?

VIRGINIA: Not at first, your Eminence. There is so much to
prepare for a wedding.

THE INQUISITOR: Ah. – So you will return with your father to
Florence. I am glad of that. I can imagine that your father
needs you. Mathematics is a cold companion, is it not? A
creature of flesh and blood in such surroundings makes all

the difference. If one is a great man it is so easy to lose oneself in the world of stars which are so very vast.

VIRGINIA *breathlessly*: You are most kind, your Eminence. Really, I understand almost nothing of such matters.

THE INQUISITOR: No? *He laughs.* In the fisherman's house they never eat fish, eh? It will amuse your father when he hears that you have in fact learnt from *me* all you know about the constellations, my child. *Leafing through the transcript*: I read here that our innovators regard our present conceptions of the importance of our dear earth as somewhat exaggerated. Now, from the days of Ptolemy, a sage of antiquity, up to the present day, it has been agreed that the width of the universe – that is the whole crystal sphere of which the earth is the centre – is about twenty thousand earth diameters. A pretty space, but too small, far too small for the innovators. According to them, so we hear, space is quite unbelievably extended. And the distance from the earth to the sun – a very considerable distance, it has always seemed to us – has become so infinitesimally small in comparison to the distance of our poor earth from the fixed stars which are attached to the very outermost sphere that it need not be taken into our calculations at all! Who could now say that the innovators do not live in a large way?

Virginia laughs. The Inquisitor laughs too.

THE INQUISITOR: In fact some gentlemen of the Holy Office have recently been almost shocked by this new picture of the universe, compared to which our accepted one is only a miniature such as could be hung round the enchanting necks of certain young ladies. They are worried because, in the case of such enormous distances, a prelate and even a cardinal might easily go astray. Even a Pope might lose the eye of the Almighty. Yes, it is funny, but I am happy to know that you will continue to be close to your father whom we all esteem so much, my dear child. I wonder whether I know your Father Confessor . . . ?

VIRGINIA: Father Christophorus from Saint Ursula.

THE INQUISITOR: Ah, yes. I am glad that you will be with your father. He will need you. You may not be able to imagine it, but it will be so. You are so young and really so very much flesh and blood, and greatness is not always easy to bear for those on whom God has bestowed it; not always. No one among mortals is so great that he cannot be included in a prayer. But now I am keeping you, dear child, and I shall be making your betrothed jealous and perhaps even your dear father, since I have been telling you something about the stars which is maybe outmoded. Now go quickly to the dancing, but do not forget to greet Father Christophorus from me.

Virginia makes a deep curtsey and goes quickly.

8

A CONVERSATION

Galileo, feeling grim,
A young monk came to visit him.
The monk was born of common folk
It was of science that they spoke.

In the Palace of the Florentine Ambassador in Rome

Galileo listens to the little monk who, after the session of the Collegium Romanum, whispered to him the verdict of the Papal astronomers.

GALILEO: Speak, speak! The habit you wear gives you the right to say whatever you wish.

THE LITTLE MONK: I have studied mathematics, Signor Galilei.

GALILEO: That might be a help, if it could induce you to admit that twice two now and again make four!

THE LITTLE MONK: Signor Galilei, for the last three nights I have been unable to sleep at all. I didn't know how to reconcile the decree which I have read and the satellites of Jupiter which I have seen. I decided to say Mass early today and then come to you.

GALILEO: In order to inform me that Jupiter has no satellites?

THE LITTLE MONK: No. I have succeeded in fathoming the wisdom
of that decree. It has revealed to me the danger to mankind
that lurks in too much uncontrolled research, and I have decided to give up astronomy. However, it is still my duty to
put before you the reasons which should cause even an astronomer to desist from further work on that particular teaching.

GALILEO: I may say that such reasons are already known to me.

THE LITTLE MONK: I understand your bitterness. You are thinking of certain exceptional powers which the Church can
command.

GALILEO: Just say instruments of torture.

THE LITTLE MONK: But I would mention other reasons. Let me
speak for a moment of myself. I grew up as a son of peasants
in the Campagna. They were simple people. They knew all
about olive-trees, but very little else. While observing the
phases of Venus, I can see my parents, sitting by the hearth
with my sister, eating their cheese. I see above them the
beams blackened by centuries of smoke, and I see clearly,
their old, work-worn hands and the little spoons they hold.
They are not rich, but even in their misfortune there lies
concealed a certain invisible order of things. There are those
various rounds of duties, from scrubbing the floor, through
the seasons in the olive grove, to the payment of taxes. There
is even regularity in the disasters that befall them. My father's
back becomes bent, not suddenly, but more and more each
spring among the olive-trees, just as the childbearings which
have made my mother less and less a woman have followed one
another at regular intervals. But they call up the strength to
sweat up the stony paths with their baskets, to bear children,
yes, even to eat, from the feeling of continuity and necessity
which is given them by the sight of the soil, of the trees
springing with new green foliage every year, of the little
church, and by listening every Sunday to the Bible texts.
They have been assured that the eye of God rests upon them;
searchingly, yes, almost anxiously – that the whole universe
has been built up round them in order that they, the actors,
can play their greater or lesser parts. What would my people

say if they learned from me that they were really on a little bit of rock that ceaselessly revolves in empty space round another star, one among very many, a comparatively unimportant one? Why is such patience, such acceptance of their misery, either necessary or good today? Why is there still virtue in Holy Writ, which explains everything and has established the necessity of toil, endurance, hunger, resignation, and which now is found to be full of errors? No, I see their eyes grow frightened! I see them dropping their spoons on the hearth-stone, I see how they feel cheated and betrayed. So there is no eye resting upon us, they say. We must look after ourselves, untaught, old and worn out as we are? No one has provided a part for us on this earthly, miserable, tiny star which is not independent and round which nothing revolves? There is no meaning in our misery, hunger is simply not-having-eaten, and not a test of strength; exertion is just stooping and tugging – with nothing to show. So do you understand that in that decree of the Holy Congregation I perceive true maternal compassion, great goodness of soul?

GALILEO: Goodness of soul! What you probably mean is – there's nothing there, the wine's drunk up, their lips are parched, so let them kiss the cassock! And why is nothing there? Why is the orderliness in this country merely the order of an empty cupboard, and the necessity merely that of working oneself to death? Among bursting vineyards, beside the ripening cornfields! Your Campagna peasants are paying for the wars which the representative of gentle Jesus is waging in Spain and Germany. Why does he put the earth at the hub of the universe? So that the throne of Saint Peter can stand at the hub of the earth. That's why! You are right; it's nothing to do with the planets, it's to do with the peasants in the Campagna. And don't come talking to me about the beauty of phenomena to which age has given a golden patina! Do you know how Margaritifera oysters produce their pearls? When suffering from a deadly disease they envelop an unbearable foreign body – a grain of sand for example – in a nacreous secretion. They nearly die in the process. To the devil with the pearls. I prefer a healthy oyster. Virtues are not linked with misery, my friend. If your people were prosperous and happy, they could develop the virtues derived of prosperity and happiness. But now these virtues come from exhausted men on exhausted acres, and I reject them. Sir, my new water-pumps can work more miracles than your ridiculous superhuman slave-driving. – 'Be fruitful and multiply', for fields are unfruitful and wars are decimating you. Should I lie to your people?

THE LITTLE MONK *in great agitation*: The very highest reasons keep us silent – the peace of mind of our unfortunate people.

GALILEO: Would you like to see a Cellini clock which Cardinal Bellarmin's coachman delivered here this morning? My friend, as a reward for leaving undisturbed the peace of mind of, shall we say, your worthy parents, the authorities offer me wine pressed with the sweat of their brows, which are said to have been created in the image of God. Were I prepared to keep silence, it would doubtless be for the basest of reasons: comfort, freedom from persecution, etc.

THE LITTLE MONK: Signor Galilei, I am a priest.

GALILEO: You are also a physicist. And you see that Venus has phases. Look through there! *He points through the window.* Do you see that little Priapus there on the well beside the laurel? The god of gardens, of birds and of thieves – rustic, obscene, two-thousand-years-old! He told fewer lies. – All right, I'm a son of the Church too. But do you know the eight satires of Horace? I've just been reading him again; he gives one a sense of balance. *He reaches out for a little book.* He lets Priapus speak, a little statue which was put up in the Esquiline Gardens. It begins like this:

'A fig-tree log, a useless piece of wood
Was I, when the carpenter, uncertain
Whether to carve a Priapus or a stool
Decided on the god . . .'

Do you think Horace would have forgone the stool and let a table be put into the poem? Sir, my sense of beauty is wounded if Venus appears in my universe without phases.

We cannot invent machinery for pumping up the water from the river if we may not study the greatest machinery that lies before our eyes, the machinery of the stars. The sum of the angles in a triangle cannot be changed according to the requirements of the Curia. I cannot calculate the paths of freely moving bodies in such a way as to explain the rides of witches upon broomsticks.

THE LITTLE MONK: And do you not believe that the truth – if it be the truth – will triumph even without us?

GALILEO: No, no, no. Truth will triumph only in so far as we triumph; the victory of reason can only be the victory of reasonable people. You describe your Campagna peasants just like the moss on their huts! How can anyone assume that the sum of the angles in a triangle could contradict *their* requirements? But if they never stir themselves and start to think, the most beautiful irrigation schemes will be of no use to them. Damnation, I perceive the divine patience of your people, but where is their divine anger?

THE LITTLE MONK: They are tired.

GALILEO *throws a bundle of manuscript to him*: Are you a physicist, my son? Here you will find the reasons why the ocean moves in ebb and flood. But you mustn't read it, do you hear. Oh, you're already reading it? So you are a physicist?

The little monk is engrossed in the papers.

GALILEO: An apple from the tree of knowledge! He's already cramming it in. He's eternally damned, but he must cram it in, an unhappy guzzler! Sometimes I think I'll have myself shut in a dungeon ten fathoms under the ground where no light penetrates, if I could thereby discover what it is – light. And the worst is that what I know I must repeat. Like a lover, like a drunkard, like a traitor. It's nothing but a sin and leads to disaster. How long shall I be able simply to shout it at the fireplace – that's the question.

THE LITTLE MONK *pointing to a passage in the papers*: I cannot understand this sentence.

GALILEO: I'll explain it to you. I'll explain it to you.

9

AFTER EIGHT YEARS OF SILENCE, THE ENTHRONEMENT OF
A NEW POPE, HIMSELF A MATHEMATICIAN, ENCOURAGES
GALILEO TO RESUME HIS RESEARCHES INTO THE FOR-
BIDDEN SUBJECT OF SUN-SPOTS

*Does not give
away what is to
happen but rather
like words at end
A map, serial —
whet ones
appetite*

Eight long years with tongue in cheek
Of what he knew he did not speak.
Then temptation grew too great
And Galileo challenged fate.

Galileo's House in Florence

*Galileo's pupils, Federzoni, the little monk and Andrea Sarti, now
a young man, are assembled for a practical lecture. Galileo himself
reads a book, standing up. Virginia and Signora Sarti are sewing the
trousseau.*

VIRGINIA: Sewing a trousseau is fun. This is for a long dining
table, Ludovico loves entertaining. It has to be very neat; his
mother notices every thread. She doesn't agree with father's
books. Like Father Christophorus.

SIGNORA SARTI: He hasn't written a new book for years.

VIRGINIA: I think he's realised he was mistaken. In Rome a very
high church dignitary explained to me a lot about astronomy.
The distances are too great.

ANDREA *as he writes up the lesson for the day on a blackboard*:
'Thursday afternoon. Floating bodies.' Ice again; a pail with
water; scales; iron needle; Aristotle.

*He fetches out the various objects. The others follow what he says
in their books. Enter Filippo Mucius, a scholar of middle age. He
has a rather agitated manner.*

MUCIUS: Can you tell Signor Galilei that he must receive me?
He damns me without hearing me.

SIGNORA SARTI: But he will *not* receive you.

MUCIUS: God will reward you if you ask him once again. I *must*
speak to him.

VIRGINIA *goes to the stairs*: Father!

GALILEO: What is it?

VIRGINIA: Signor Mucius.

GALILEO *standing up abruptly, goes to the top of the stairs, his pupils behind him*: What do you want?

MUCIUS: Signor Galilei, I beg you will permit me to explain to you those passages in my book where there appears to be disproof of the Copernican teaching about the rotation of the earth. I have . . .

GALILEO: What are you trying to explain? You are in agreement with the decree of the Holy Congregation of 1616. You are entirely within your rights. You have certainly studied mathematics here, but that imposes on us no obligation to hear from you that twice two makes four. You are, on the other hand, perfectly entitled to say that this stone – *he takes a little stone from his pocket and throws it on the floor* – has just flown up into the roof.

MUCIUS: Signor Galilei, I . . .

GALILEO: Don't talk about difficulties! I didn't let the plague stop me from continuing with my researches.

MUCIUS: Signor Galilei, the plague is not the worst thing.

GALILEO: I say to you: he who does not know the truth is merely an idiot. But he who knows it and calls it a lie, is a criminal. Get out of my house!

MUCIUS *tonelessly*: You are right. *He goes.*

Galileo goes back to his study.

FEDERZONI: Unfortunately, that's the trouble. He is not a great man and would be of no importance were it not that he has been your pupil. But now, of course, people will say: he's heard everything that Galilei teaches and he has to admit that it is all false.

SIGNORA SARTI: I am sorry for the gentleman.

VIRGINIA: Father was too fond of him.

SIGNORA SARTI: I would like to talk to you about your marriage, Virginia. You're still such a young thing, and you have no mother, and your father floats these bits of ice on water. Anyway, I wouldn't advise you to ask *him* anything about your marriage. He'd take a whole week-end and at mealtime and when young people are at table he'd say the most shocking things, not having half a scudo's worth of modesty – he never had. And I don't mean things like that; simply, what the future holds for you. I can't know such things; I'm an uneducated person. But one doesn't go blindly into a serious situation like marriage. I mean, really you ought to go to a proper astronomer at the University, so that he can cast your horoscope, when you'll know where you are. What are you laughing at?

VIRGINIA: Because I did go to him.

SIGNORA SARTI *very curious*: What did he say?

VIRGINIA: For three months I must be careful because the sun will be in Capricorn, but after that I'll have an extremely favourable ascendent and the clouds will part. If I don't let Jupiter out of sight, I can undertake any journey I fancy, since I'm a Capricorn.

SIGNORA SARTI: And Ludovico?

VIRGINIA: He's a Leo. *After a slight pause.* His nature is sensual. *A pause.* I know that step. It is the Rector, Signor Gaffone.

Enter Signor Gaffone, Rector of the University.

GAFFONE: I'm only bringing a book that may interest your father. Please, for Heaven's sake, don't disturb Signor Galilei. I cannot help it, but I always feel that every minute stolen from that great man is a minute stolen from Italy. I'll put the book, in mint condition, into your hands and steal away on tip-toe.

He leaves. Virginia gives the book to Federzoni.

GALILEO: What's it about?

FEDERZONI: I don't know. *He spells it out.* 'De Maculis in Sole.'

ANDREA: On sun-spots. Another one!

Federzoni hands it over to him crossly.

ANDREA: Listen to the dedication! 'To the greatest living authority on physics, Galileo Galilei.'

Galileo has already immersed himself again in his book.

ANDREA: I've already read the sun-spot treatise by Fabricius of Holland. He believes they are swarms of stars passing between the earth and the sun.

THE LITTLE MONK: Isn't that rather doubtful, Signor Galilei?

Galileo does not answer.

ANDREA: In Paris and Prague they believe they are vapours from the sun.

FEDERZONI: Hm.

ANDREA: Federzoni doubts that.

FEDERZONI: Please leave me out of it. I have said 'Hm', that's all. I'm a lens-grinder. I grind lenses, and you look through them and observe the heavens, and what you see are not spots but 'maculis'. How could I ever doubt anything? How often must I keep saying to you that I can't read books, they're all in Latin.

In fury he gesticulates with the scales. A pan falls to the floor. Galileo goes across and silently picks it up.

THE LITTLE MONK: There is joy in doubt. I wonder why?

ANDREA: For the last two weeks, on every sunny day, I've climbed up into the attic under the roof. Through a tiny crack in the shingles falls just a thin ray of light. And that way one can get a reversed image of the sun on a sheet of paper. I have seen a spot, as big as a fly, swept away like a cloudlet. It wandered, too. Why don't we investigate the spots, Signor Galilei?

GALILEO: Because we are working on floating bodies.

ANDREA: Mother has wash-baskets full of letters. All Europe is asking for your opinion. Your reputation has grown so great that you cannot remain silent.

GALILEO: Rome has permitted my reputation to grow because I have remained silent.

FEDERZONI: But now you can no longer afford to be silent.

GALILEO: Neither can I afford to allow myself to be smoked over a wood-fire like a ham.

ANDREA: Do you think these spots have anything to do with this matter?

Galileo does not answer.

ANDREA: All right, let's keep to our bits of ice; they can't do you any harm.

GALILEO: Correct. – Our thesis, Andrea!

ANDREA: As far as the property of floating is concerned, let us assume that it is not the shape of a body that matters, but whether it is lighter or heavier than water.

GALILEO: What does Aristotle say?

THE LITTLE MONK: 'Discus latus platique . . .'

GALILEO: Translate, translate!

THE LITTLE MONK: 'A broad and flat disc of ice is able to float on water, whereas an iron needle sinks.'

GALILEO: Why, according to Aristotle, does the ice not sink?

THE LITTLE MONK: Because it is broad and flat and so is unable to divide the water.

GALILEO: Good. *He takes up a lump of ice and places it in the pail of water.* Now I press the ice forcibly down to the bottom of the vessel. I remove the pressure of my hands. And what happens?

THE LITTLE MONK: It rises to the surface again.

GALILEO: Right. Apparently it can divide the water when rising. – Fulganzio!

THE LITTLE MONK: But then why does it float at all? It is heavier than water because it is condensed water.

GALILEO: What if it were thinned water?

ANDREA: It must be lighter than water, otherwise it wouldn't float.

GALILEO: Aha!

ANDREA: Just as an iron needle won't float. Everything that's lighter than water floats, and everything that's heavier sinks. Quod erat demonstrandum.

GALILEO: Andrea, you must learn to think carefully. Give me the needle. A sheet of paper. Is iron heavier than water?

ANDREA: Yes.

Galileo lays the needle on the sheet of paper and then gently slides the needle on to the surface of the water. A pause.

GALILEO: What has happened?

FEDERZONI: The needle is floating! Holy Aristotle, they've never put him to the test! *They laugh.*

GALILEO: One of the chief causes of poverty in science is usually imaginary wealth. The aim of science is not to open a door to infinite wisdom, but to set a limit to infinite error. – Make your notes.

VIRGINIA: What is it?

SIGNORA SARTI: Every time they laugh, it gives me a little shudder. What are they laughing at, I wonder.

VIRGINIA: Father says: the theologians have their bell-ringing, and the physicists have their laughter.

SIGNORA SARTI: But I'm glad that at least he no longer looks through his telescope so often.

VIRGINIA: Now he's only putting pieces of ice into water; not much harm can come of that.

SIGNORA SARTI: I don't know.

Enter Ludovico in travelling clothes, followed by a servant carrying pieces of luggage. Virginia runs over to him and embraces him.

VIRGINIA: Why didn't you write to me that you were coming?

LUDOVICO: I was near by, visiting our vineyards at Bucciole, and I couldn't keep away from you.

GALILEO *as if short-sighted*: Who is that?

VIRGINIA: Ludovico.

THE LITTLE MONK: Can't you see him?

GALILEO: Oh, yes, Ludovico. *He walks towards him.* How are the horses?

LUDOVICO: They are doing well, signor.

GALILEO: Sarti, we'll have a celebration. Fetch a jug of that Sicilian wine, the old wine.

Exit Signora Sarti with Andrea.

LUDOVICO *to Virginia*: You look pale. Living in the country will suit you. Mother is expecting you in September.

VIRGINIA: Wait – I'll show you my wedding-dress. *She runs out.*

GALILEO: Sit down.

LUDOVICO: I hear you have more than a thousand students at your lectures in the University, signor. What are you working on at the moment?

GALILEO: The same sort of thing, day after day. Have you come through Rome?

LUDOVICO: Yes. – Before I forget it, Mother congratulates you on your admirable tact over the new sun-spot orgies of the Dutch.

GALILEO *drily*: Thank you.

Signora Sarti and Andrea bring in wine and glasses. All settle round the table.

LUDOVICO: Rome's already got its topic of conversation for February. Father Christopher Clavius has expressed a fear that the whole earth-round-the-sun hullabaloo may be started up again by these sun-spots.

ANDREA: No need to worry.

GALILEO: Any further gossip in the Holy City, apart from hopes of new sins on my part?

LUDOVICO: You know, of course, that the Holy Father is dying?

THE LITTLE MONK: Oh!

GALILEO: Who is mentioned as his successor?

LUDOVICO: Most people say Barberini.

GALILEO: Barberini.

ANDREA: Signor Galilei knows Barberini.

THE LITTLE MONK: Cardinal Barberini is a mathematician.

FEDERZONI: A man of science on the Papal Throne!

GALILEO: Well, nowadays they need men like Barberini, who have read a bit of mathematics. Things are starting to move, Federzoni; we may yet live to see the day when we no longer have to look over our shoulders like criminals when we say that twice two is four. *To Ludovico*: I admire this wine, Ludovico. What do you think of it?

LUDOVICO: It's good.

GALILEO: I know the vineyard. The slope is steep and stony, the grapes almost blue. I love its wine.

LUDOVICO: Yes, signor.

GALILEO: It has little shadows in it. And it is almost sweet, but one mustn't forget the 'almost'. – Andrea, clear that stuff away, the ice, the pail and the needle. – I enjoy the consolations of the flesh. I have no patience with cowardly souls who call them little weaknesses. I say: enjoyment is an accomplishment.

THE LITTLE MONK: What are you proposing to do?

FEDERZONI: We'll begin again with the earth-round-the-sun hullabaloo.

ANDREA *humming*:

> The Bible says the earth stands still, my dears
> A fact which every learned doctor proves:
> The Holy Father grabs it by the ears
> And holds it hard and fast. – And yet it moves.

Andrea, Federzoni and the little monk hurry across to the experimental table and clear it.

ANDREA: We might find out that the sun itself revolves. How would you like that, Marsili?

LUDOVICO: Why the excitement?

SIGNORA SARTI: You aren't going to start again with all that devil's stuff, Signor Galilei?

GALILEO: I know now why your mother sent you to me. Barberini in the ascendent! Knowledge will become a passion, and research a pleasure. Clavius is right; these sun-spots interest me. Do you like my wine, Ludovico?

LUDOVICO: I've told you so, signor.

GALILEO: You really like it?

LUDOVICO *stiffly*: I like it.

GALILEO: Would you go so far as to accept a man's wine or his daughter without demanding that he abandons his calling? What has my astronomy to do with my daughter? The phases of Venus don't affect her curves.

SIGNORA SARTI: Don't be so vulgar. I'll fetch Virginia right away.

LUDOVICO *holds her back*: Marriages in families like mine are not made only from the sexual point of view.

GALILEO: Did they restrain you from marrying my daughter for eight years, while I had to serve a probation period?

LUDOVICO: My wife will also have to cut a figure in our place in the village church.

GALILEO: You mean, your peasants will make it dependent upon the godliness of their squire's wife whether they pay their rents or not.

LUDOVICO: In a manner of speaking.

GALILEO: Andrea, Fulganzio, fetch the brass reflector and the screen. We'll throw the picture of the sun on to it to spare our eyes; that's your method, Andrea.

Andrea and the little monk fetch the reflector and screen.

LUDOVICO: In Rome, at that time, you signed that you wouldn't meddle any more in that earth-round-the-sun business, signor.

GALILEO: Oh, then! Then we had a reactionary Pope!

SIGNORA SARTI: Had! And His Holiness isn't yet dead!

GALILEO: Almost, almost. – Lay a squared grid over the screen. We'll proceed methodically. And then we'll be able to answer their letters, won't we, Andrea?

SIGNORA SARTI: 'Almost!' Fifty times the man re-weighs his lumps of ice, but when it's something that suits his stomach he swallows it blind.

The screen is set up.

LUDOVICO: Should His Holiness die, Signor Galilei, the next Pope, whoever he may be and however great his love for science, will also have to pay due regard to the extent of the love which the foremost families in the land feel towards him.

THE LITTLE MONK: God made the physical world, Ludovico; God made the human brain; God will permit physics.

SIGNORA SARTI: Galileo, now I'll tell *you* something. I have seen my son fall into sin over these 'Experiments' and 'Theories' and 'Observations', and I haven't been able to do anything. You have set yourself up against the authorities and they have already warned you once. The most eminent cardinals have talked to you like a sick beast. It worked for a time, but two months ago, soon after the Annunciation, I caught you again, starting up secretly with those 'Observations'. In the attic! I didn't say much, but I knew all right. I ran out and lit a candle to Saint Joseph. It was beyond me. When I'm alone with you, you show signs of sense and tell me that you know you must control yourself because it's dangerous, but two days' experimenting and you're as bad as ever. If I have to give up my eternal salvation for sticking to a heretic, that's my business, but you've no right to trample on your daughter's happiness with your great flat feet.

GALILEO *peevishly*: Bring the telescope.

LUDOVICO: Giuseppe, put my luggage back in the coach.

Exit the servant.

SIGNORA SARTI: She won't get over that! You can tell her yourself!

She runs off, still holding the jug.

LUDOVICO: I see you have already made your preparations. Signor Galilei, my mother and I spend three quarters of the year on our estate in the Campagna, and we can assure you that your treatises on the satellites of Jupiter in no way disturb our peasants. Their work in the fields is too arduous. Yet it could disturb them to learn that frivolous attacks on the sacred doctrines of the Church now go unpunished. Don't entirely forget that these unfortunates, in their animal-like condition, get everything confused. They really *are* animals. You can scarcely conceive it. At the rumour that an apple-tree's bearing pears they'll run away from the fields to gossip about it.

GALILEO *interested*: Will they?

LUDOVICO: Animals. When they come to our house to complain about some trivial thing, mother's compelled to have a hound whipped before their eyes; that's the only thing that will remind them of breeding and behaviour and civility. You, Signor Galilei, occasionally see from a travelling coach fruitful fields of maize; absent-mindedly you eat our olives and our cheese; and you have no idea what trouble, what supervision it takes to grow these things.

GALILEO: Young man, I do not eat my olives absent-mindedly. *Angrily.* You're detaining me. *He calls upstairs.* Have you got the screen?

ANDREA: Yes. Are you coming?

GALILEO: It's not only hounds you whip to keep them under control, eh Marsili?

LUDOVICO: Signor Galilei. You have a wonderful brain. A pity.

THE LITTLE MONK *amazed*: He's threatening you.

GALILEO: Yes. I might stir up his peasants into thinking new thoughts. And his servants and his stewards.

FEDERZONI: How? None of them reads Latin.

GALILEO: I could write for the many in the language of the people, instead of in Latin for the few. For these new ideas we need people who work with their hands. Who else wants to learn about the origins of things? Those who see only the bread on the table don't want to know how it is baked; that lot would rather thank God above than the baker. But those who make the bread will understand that nothing moves which isn't moved. Your sister at the olive-press, Fulganzio, will not be greatly amazed, but will probably laugh when she hears that the sun is not a golden coat of arms but a lever; the earth moves, because the sun moves it.

LUDOVICO: You will always be the slave of your own infatuations. Excuse me to Virginia; I think it is better not to see her now.

GALILEO: The dowry is at your disposal at any time.

LUDOVICO: Good day. *He goes.*

ANDREA: And give our regards to all the Marsilis!

FEDERZONI: Who command the earth to stand still so that their castles don't come tumbling down!

ANDREA: And the Cencis and the Villanis!

FEDERZONI: The Cervillis!

ANDREA: The Lecchis!

FEDERZONI: The Pirleonis!

ANDREA: Who are only willing to kiss the Pope's feet if he'll trample down the people with them.

THE LITTLE MONK *now at the apparatus*: The new Pope will be an enlightened man.

GALILEO: So now we start on our observation of these spots on the sun, which interest us, at our own risk and without counting too much on the protection of a new Pope.

ANDREA *interrupting*: But with full confidence in dispersing the star-shadows of Signor Fabricius and the sun-vapours of Prague and Paris, and of proving the rotation of the sun.

GALILEO: With some confidence in proving the rotation of the sun. My intention is not to prove that hitherto I have been right; but to discover whether I am right. I say: abandon all hope, you who enter the realm of observation. Perhaps they are clouds, perhaps they are spots, but before we assume that they are spots, which would be most opportune for us, let us rather assume that they are fishes' tails. Yes, we will question everything, everything once again. And we shall advance not in seven-league boots, but at a snail's pace. And what we find today we shall strike out from the record tomorrow, and only write it in again when we have once more discovered it. And what we wish to find, if we do find it, we shall regard with especial distrust. So we shall start our observations of the sun with the inexorable determination to prove that the earth *stands still*. Only when we are defeated, utterly and hopelessly defeated, and are licking our wounds in the most miserable dejection, shall we begin to ask ourselves whether we may be right after all and perhaps the earth does move! *With a wink.* And if every conception but this one goes up in smoke, then there can be no more mercy for those who have not searched and yet speak. Take the cloth off the telescope and turn it to the sun.

He sets up the brass reflector.

THE LITTLE MONK: I knew that you had already begun your work. I knew it when you didn't recognise Signor Marsili.

Silently they begin their observations. When the flaming image of the

*sun appears on the screen, Virginia comes running in in her wedding-
dress.*

VIRGINIA: You sent him away, father!

She faints. Andrea and the little monk run over to her.

GALILEO: I've got to know the truth.

10

DURING THE FOLLOWING DECADE GALILEO'S TEACHING
SPREADS AMONG THE PEOPLE. PAMPHLETEERS AND
BALLAD-SINGERS EVERYWHERE TAKE UP THE NEW IDEAS.
IN 1632, DURING CARNIVAL TIME, MANY CITIES IN ITALY
CHOOSE ASTRONOMY AS THE THEME FOR THE GUILDS'
PROCESSIONS

> On April Fool's Day, 'thirty two,
> Of science there was much ado,
> People had learned from Galilei:
> They used his teaching in their way.

A Marketplace

*A half-starved pair of strolling players with a five-year-old girl and
a baby enter a marketplace where a crowd, many masked, are waiting
for the carnival procession. Both carry bundles, a drum and assorted
utensils.*

THE BALLAD-SINGER *drumming*: Esteemed citizens, ladies and
gentlemen! Before the great carnival procession of the guilds
arrives, we bring you the latest song from Florence, a song
which is being sung throughout the whole of Upper Italy
and which we have imported here at great cost. It is entitled:
*The Terrible Teachings and Views of Court Physicist Signor
Galileo Galilei, or a Foretaste of the Future.*
He sings:
> When the Almighty ordered his great Creation,
> He told the sun that it, at his command,
> Must circle round the earth for illumination
> Just like a little maiden, lamp in hand.

For it was His desire each thing inferior
Should henceforth circle round its own superior.
And things began to turn for all their worth
The lesser ones around the greater
And round the earlier the later,
As it is in Heaven so on earth.
And round the Pope revolve the cardinals
And round the cardinals revolve the bishops
And round the bishops revolve the secretaries
And round the secretaries revolve the magistrates
And round the magistrates revolve the craftsmen
And round the craftsmen revolve the servants
And round the servants revolve the dogs, the chickens and
   the beggars.

That, good people, is the Great Order, ordo ordinum as the
Signori theologians say, regula aeternis, the Rule of Rules –
but what, dear people, happened?

He sings:

Then up got Doctor Galilei
(Threw the Bible away, caught up his telescope,
   Took a look at the universe.)
   'Stand still!' to the sun he said,
   'For now the Creatio Dei
   Shall turn the opposite way.
   Now the mistress must obey
   And turn around her maid.'
You say that's scandalous? Good people, that's no jest.
The serving folk grow bolder every day. – Disaster!
Yet one thing's true: life's dull for you. And hand on breast,
Who wouldn't rather be his own liege lord and master?

Worthy citizens, such teachings are quite impossible.

He sings:

         An idle lad, a cheeky lass
         The hounds all overfed –
         The choirboy comes no more to Mass
         The apprentice lies abed.

No, no, no! With the Bible do not jest!
If the rope round our neck isn't thick it'll break. – Disaster!
Yet one thing's true: life's dull for you. And hand on breast:
Who wouldn't be his own liege lord and master?

Good people, cast a glance into the future as the learned
Doctor Galileo Galilei predicts it:

He sings:

> Two housewives stand in the market square
> Not knowing which way to turn;
> The fishwife pulls out a loaf right there
> And eats her fish alone!
> The mason digs his plot with care
> And takes the builder's stone
> And when the house is finished and fair
> Why! he moves in on his own!

But can this be allowed? No, no, it is no jest.
If the rope around our neck isn't thick it'll break. – Disaster!
Yet one thing's true; life's dull for you. And hand on breast:
Who wouldn't rather be his own true lord and master?

> The farmer kicks the landlord
> And attacks him with his scythe
> While the farmer's wife gives her children
> Milk from the parson's tithe.

No, no, good people, with the Bible do not jest!
If the rope round our neck isn't thick it'll break. – Disaster!
Yet one thing's true; life's dull for you. And hand on breast:
Who wouldn't be his own liege lord and master?

THE SINGER'S WOMAN:

> I've just kicked over the traces
> For I said to my man, said I:
> A fixed star from other places
> Might do better than you. – I'll try.

THE SINGER:

> No, no, no, no! Stop, Galileo, stop it all!
> Unmuzzle a mad dog and he'll bite. – Disaster!
> Of course it's true: fun and games are too few and duties call:
> Who wouldn't rather be his own lord and master?

BOTH:

> All you who live on earth in wretchedness
> Arise! Stir up your feeble spirits faster
> And learn from worthy Doctor Galuliss
> The wondrous A.B.C. of earthly bliss
> Only obedience holds us back from this!
> Who wouldn't rather be his own liege lord and master?

THE SINGER: Esteemed citizens, behold Galileo Galilei's phenomenal discovery: The earth circling round the sun!

He pounds fiercely on his drum. The woman and the child step forward. The woman carries a crude representation of the sun, and the child, holding a pumpkin above its head to represent the earth, circles round the woman. The singer points triumphantly at the child, as if it were executing some perilous death-defying feat as it walks jerkily, step by step, in time to single taps on the drum. There is a roll of drums from the back.

A DEEP VOICE *calls out*: The procession!

Enter two men in rags, pulling a little cart. On a ridiculous throne sits 'The Grand Duke of Florence', a figure in a pasteboard crown and clothed in sacking and peering through a telescope. Above the throne is a signboard: 'Looking out for Trouble'. Then four masked men march in, carrying a huge baldachin. They stop and toss into the air a dummy representing a cardinal. A dwarf has established himself at one side with a board bearing the words 'The New Age'. In the crowd a beggar raises himself on his crutch and stamps on the ground, dancing, until he falls down with a crash. Enter an over-life-size dummy, Galileo Galilei, who bows to the public. In front of it a child carries a gigantic Bible, open, with the pages crossed out.

THE BALLAD-SINGER: Galileo Galilei, the Bible-buster!

Tremendous laughter from the crowd.

11

1633: THE INQUISITION SUMMONS THE WORLD-FAMOUS SCHOLAR TO ROME

> The depths are hot, the heights are chill
> The streets are loud, the court is still.

Lobby and staircase of the Medici Palace in Florence

Galileo and his daughter are waiting to be admitted to the Grand Duke.

VIRGINIA: It's taking a long time.

GALILEO: Yes.

VIRGINIA: There's that man again, the one who followed us here.
She points to an individual who passes without looking at them.

GALILEO *whose sight has deteriorated*: I do not know him.

VIRGINIA: But I have often seen him during the last few days.
He makes me uneasy.

GALILEO: Nonsense. We are in Florence and not among Corsican bandits.

VIRGINIA: Here comes Rector Gaffone.

GALILEO: He's the one I'm afraid of. The fool will involve me in another hour-long conversation.

Down the stairs comes Signor Gaffone, the Rector of the University. He is visibly alarmed when he sees Galileo and, with his head sharply averted, he walks past the pair, scarcely nodding.

GALILEO: What has got into him? My eyes are bad again today.
Did he greet us at all?

VIRGINIA: Hardly. – What is in your book? Is it possible they think it heretical?

GALILEO: You hang around in churches too much. All this getting up early and going to Mass is completely ruining your complexion. You pray for me, don't you?

VIRGINIA: Here is Signor Vanni, the iron-founder you designed that smelting plant for. Don't forget to thank him for the quails.

A man is coming down the staircase.

VANNI: Did you enjoy the quails I sent you, Signor Galilei?

GALILEO: The quails were excellent, Master Vanni. Again, my best thanks.

VANNI: They were talking about you upstairs. They are holding you responsible for those pamphlets against the Bible which have lately been on sale everywhere.

GALILEO: I know nothing about pamphlets. The Bible and Homer are my favourite reading.

VANNI: And even if that were not so, I should like to take this opportunity of assuring you that we manufacturers are on your side. I am not a man who knows much about the movements of the stars, but to me you are the man who fights for the freedom to teach new things. Take that mechanical cultivator from Germany which you described to me. Last year alone five books on agriculture were published in London. We here would be only too thankful for a book on Dutch canals. The very same circles that are making difficulties for you will not permit the doctors of Bologna to dissect corpses for purposes of research.

GALILEO: Your opinion carries weight, Vanni.

VANNI: I hope so. Do you know that in Amsterdam and London they have money markets? Also trade schools. And papers appearing regularly with the latest news. Here we haven't even the liberty to make money. They are against iron-foundries because they believe too many workers together in one place will encourage immorality! I stand and fall with men like you, Signor Galilei. If they ever try to do anything against you, I beg you to remember that you have friends throughout the world of commerce. Behind you stand the cities of Upper Italy, Signor Galilei.

GALILEO: So far as I know, nobody intends to do anything against me.

VANNI: No?

GALILEO: No.

VANNI: In my opinion you would be better off in Venice. Fewer blackcoats. From there you could take up the fight. I have a travelling-coach and horses, Signor Galilei.

GALILEO: I cannot see myself as a refugee. I value my comfort.

VANNI: Of course. But after what I've heard upstairs here, it's a matter of haste. I have the impression they would rather you weren't in Florence just now.

GALILEO: Nonsense. The Grand Duke is my pupil, and besides, the Pope himself would counter any attempt to entrap me with a forceful No!

VANNI: You seem unable to distinguish your friends from your enemies, Signor Galilei.

GALILEO: I know the difference between power and impotence.

He walks brusquely away.

VANNI: Very well. I wish you luck.

Exit.

GALILEO *returns to Virginia*: Every Tom, Dick and Harry here with any sort of grievance picks me for his spokesman, particularly in places where it's not likely to do me any good. I have written a book about the mechanics of the universe, that's all. What is made or not made of it is no concern of mine.

VIRGINIA *loudly*: If only people knew how you condemned what happened everywhere last carnival.

GALILEO: Yes. Give a bear honey, and you'll lose your arm if the beast is hungry!

VIRGINIA *softly*: Did the Grand Duke actually summon you here today?

GALILEO: No, but I had myself announced. He wants to have the book; he has paid for it. Ask that official, and complain about them keeping us waiting here.

VIRGINIA *followed by the individual, goes over to speak to an official*: Signor Mincio, has his Highness been informed that my father wishes to speak with him?

THE OFFICIAL: How should I know?

VIRGINIA: That is no answer.

THE OFFICIAL: No?

VIRGINIA: It is your business to be polite.

The official half turns his back on her and yawns, looking at the individual.

VIRGINIA *returns*: He says the Grand Duke is still busy.

GALILEO: I heard you say something about 'polite'. What was it?

VIRGINIA: I thanked him for his polite reply, that was all. Can't you leave the book here? You are only wasting your time.

GALILEO: I am beginning to ask myself what my time is worth. Possibly I might accept Sagredo's invitation to go to Padua for a few weeks. My health is not too good.

VIRGINIA: You couldn't live without your books.

GALILEO: I could take a cask or two of the Sicilian wine in the coach.

VIRGINIA: You've always said it won't stand travelling. And the Court still owes you three months' salary. They won't send it after you.

GALILEO: That's true.

The Cardinal Inquisitor comes down the stairs.

VIRGINIA: The Cardinal Inquisitor.

In passing he bows deeply to Galileo.

VIRGINIA: What is the Cardinal Inquisitor doing in Florence, Father?

GALILEO: I don't know. He behaved not unrespectfully. I knew what I was doing when I came to Florence and kept silence all those years. They praised me so highly that now they must accept me as I am.

THE OFFICIAL *calls out*: His Highness the Grand Duke!

Cosimo de' Medici comes down the stairs. Galileo goes up to him. Cosimo stops, slightly embarrassed.

GALILEO: I wish to show your Highness my dialogues on the two greatest astronomical systems . . .

COSIMO: Aha, aha! How are your eyes?

GALILEO: Not at their best, your Highness. If your Highness permits, I have the book . . .

COSIMO: The condition of your eyes worries me. Really, it worries

me. It shows that you are perhaps using your excellent telescope a little too zealously, eh?

He walks on without accepting the book.

GALILEO: He didn't take my book, eh?

VIRGINIA: Father, I'm afraid.

GALILEO *sotto voce and firmly*: Don't show your feelings. From
here we will not go home, but to Volpi, the glasscutter. I have
an arrangement with him that, in the tavern yard next door
to him, there will always be a waggon with empty wine-casks
waiting to take me out of the city . . .

VIRGINIA: You knew . . .

GALILEO: Don't look round . . .

They start to leave.

A HIGH OFFICIAL *comes down the stairs*: Signor Galilei, it is my
duty to inform you that the Florentine Court is no longer
able to refuse the request of the Holy Inquisition to examine
you in Rome. The coach of the Holy Inquisition awaits you,
Signor Galilei.

12

THE POPE

An Apartment in the Vatican

*Pope Urban VIII, formerly Cardinal Barberini, has received the
Cardinal Inquisitor. During the audience he is being robed. Outside
is the sound of many shuffling feet.*

THE POPE *very loudly*: No! No! No!

THE INQUISITOR: Your Holiness, there are assembled here doctors of all faculties, representatives of all the holy orders and
of the whole priesthood who have come, with their childlike
faith in the Word of God as revealed in the Scriptures, to
receive from your Holiness the confirmation of their faith.

Will your Holiness now tell them that the Scriptures can no
longer be regarded as true?

THE POPE: I will not have the mathematical tables destroyed.
No!

THE INQUISITOR: That it is the mathematical tables and not the
spirit of denial and doubt – so say *these* people. But it is not
the tables. A terrible unrest has come into the world. It is
this unrest in their own minds which these men would im-
pose on the motionless earth. They cry: the figures compel
us! But whence come their figures? They come from doubt,
as everyone knows. These men doubt everything. Are we to
establish human society on doubt and no longer on faith?
'You are my master, but I doubt if that is a good thing.'
'That is your house and your wife, but I doubt whether they
should not be mine.' On the other hand, your Holiness's love
of art, which we have to thank for such beautiful collections,
is treated to abusive remarks daubed on the walls of Roman
houses, such as: 'What the barbarians left in Rome, the
Barberinis have plundered.' And abroad? It has pleased God
to beset the Holy See with heavy trials. Your Holiness's
Spanish policy is not understood by men who, lacking in-
sight, regret our rupture with the Emperor. For the last fifteen years Germany has been a slaughterhouse where men
have butchered one another with Biblical texts on their lips.
And now, when plague, war and the Reformation have re-
duced Christianity to a few small outposts, the rumour is
spreading through Europe that you have made a secret alliance
with the Lutheran Swedes in order to weaken the Catholic
Emperor. And these worms of mathematicians turn their
telescopes to the skies and tell the world that your Holiness
here too – in the one domain where no one has yet contested
you – is ill informed. One might think: what sudden interest
in such an obscure science as astronomy! Is it not all the
same how these spheres move? But no one in the whole of
Italy – where everyone down to the stable-boys chatters
about the phases of Venus as a result of the wicked example
of this Florentine – there is no one in Italy who does not

think at the same time of so many things which the schools and other authorities have declared to be beyond question, and which have become a burden. What would happen if all these people, so weak in the flesh and inclined towards every excess, were to believe only in their own commonsense which this madman declares to be the sole court of appeal! From first questioning whether the sun stood still over Gibeon, they might then practise their filthy doubts upon the Collects! Since they have been sailing over the ocean – I have nothing against that – they have put their faith in a brass ball they call a compass, instead of in God. Even as a young man this Galilei wrote about machines. With machines they would perform miracles. What sort of miracles? At all events, they no longer have any need of God, so what sort of miracles could these be? For example, they say there is to be no more Upper and Lower. They no longer need it. Aristotle, who in all other respects is a dead dog to them, has said – and they quote this – 'When the weaver's shuttle weaves on its own and the zither plays of itself, then the masters will need no apprentices and the rulers no servants'. And they think they have got that far. This wicked man knows what he is doing when he writes his astronomical works, not in Latin, but in the language of the fishwives and wool merchants.

THE POPE: That shows very bad taste; I will mention it to him.

THE INQUISITOR: He incites the former and bribes the latter. The seaport cities of Upper Italy are more and more insistent on having Galilei's star-charts for their ships. One will have to accede to them in this, for there are material interests at stake.

THE POPE: But these star-charts are based on his heretical assertions. It is precisely a matter of those very star-movements which are *not* possible if we reject his teachings. One cannot damn the teachings and keep the star-charts.

THE INQUISITOR: Why not? One cannot do otherwise.

THE POPE: Those footsteps make me nervous. Forgive me if I am always listening to them.

THE INQUISITOR: Perhaps they say more to you than I can, your

Holiness. Are all these to leave here with doubt in their hearts?

THE POPE: After all, the man is the greatest physicist of the age, the glory of Italy, and not just some scatter-brained fool. He has friends. There is Versailles. There is the Court at Vienna. They will call the Holy Church a sink of decayed prejudices. Hands off him!

THE INQUISITOR: In practice one would not have to go very far with him. He is a carnal man. He would succumb immediately.

THE POPE: He knows more pleasures than any other man I have met. He even thinks from sensuality. To an old wine or a new idea, he cannot say no. And I want no condemnation of physical facts, no battle-cries like: 'Here the Church, there Reason!' I have permitted him his book, so long as in conclusion it states that the last word is not with science but with faith. And he has kept to that.

THE INQUISITOR: But how? In his book a stupid man, who naturally represents the views of Aristotle, argues with a clever man, who equally naturally puts forward the opinions of Galileo; and who speaks the conclusion, your Holiness?

THE POPE: What is it now? Well, who speaks for us?

THE INQUISITOR: Not the clever man.

THE POPE: That is certainly an impertinence. This tramping in the corridors is intolerable. Is the whole world coming here?

THE INQUISITOR: Not the whole world, but its best part.

Pause. The Pope is now in his full robes.

THE POPE: The very most that may be done is to show him the instruments.

THE INQUISITOR: That will suffice, your Holiness. Signor Galilei is an expert on instruments.

13

ON THE 22ND OF JUNE, 1633, BEFORE THE INQUISITION,
GALILEO GALILEI RECANTS HIS TEACHING ABOUT THE
MOVEMENT OF THE EARTH

> June twenty-second, sixteen thirty-three.
> A momentous date for you and me.
> Of all the days that was the one
> An age of reason could have begun.

In the Palace of the Florentine Ambassador in Rome

*Galileo's pupils are waiting for news. The little monk and Federzoni
are playing the new form of chess with its extended moves. In a
corner Virginia is kneeling and praying.*

THE LITTLE MONK: The Pope has not received him. No more
scientific discussions.

FEDERZONI: He was his last hope. It was true what he said years
ago in Rome, when he was still Cardinal Barberini: 'We need
you.' Now they have him.

ANDREA: They will destroy him. The Discorsi will never be
finished.

FEDERZONI *looks at him furtively*: Do you think so?

ANDREA: Because he will never recant.

Pause.

THE LITTLE MONK: You always get distracted with trivial
thoughts when you lie awake at nights. Last night, for example, I kept thinking: he should never have left the Republic.

ANDREA: He could not write his book there.

FEDERZONI: And in Florence he could not publish it.

Pause.

THE LITTLE MONK: I also wondered whether they would leave
him his little stone which he always carries round with him
in his pocket. His touch-stone.

FEDERZONI: To that place where they are taking him, one goes
without pockets.

ANDREA *shouting*: They won't dare! And even if they do it to him, he would never recant. 'He who does not know the truth is merely an idiot, but he who knows it and calls it a lie, is a criminal.'

FEDERZONI: I do not think he will, either; and I would rather not live if he did; but they have force on their side.

ANDREA: Not everything can be accomplished by force.

FEDERZONI: Perhaps not.

THE LITTLE MONK *softly*: He has been in prison for twenty-three days. Yesterday was the great cross-examination. And today is the sitting. *Loudly, since Andrea is listening*. The time when I visited him here two days after the decree, we sat over there, and he pointed out to me the little figure of Priapus by the sundial in the garden – you can see it from here – and he compared his work to a poem by Horace in which nothing can be changed either. He spoke of his feeling for beauty, which made him search for the truth. And he quoted a motto: hieme et aestate, et prope et procul, usque dum vivam et ultra. And he meant the truth.

ANDREA *to the little monk*: Have you told him how he stood in the Collegium Romanum when they were testing his telescope? Tell him. *The little monk shakes his head*. He behaved just as usual. He stood with his hands on his buttocks, stuck out his stomach and said: 'I ask only for commonsense, gentlemen!' *Laughing, he imitates Galileo*.

Pause.

ANDREA *speaking of Virginia*: She is praying that he will recant.

FEDERZONI: Leave her. She is almost out of her mind since they spoke to her. They have summoned her Father Confessor from Florence.

Enter the individual from the Grand Duke's Palace in Florence.

THE INDIVIDUAL: Signor Galilei will soon be here. He may require a bed.

FEDERZONI: Has he been released?

THE INDIVIDUAL: It is expected that, at five o'clock at a session of the Inquisition, Signor Galilei will recant. The great bell of St. Mark's will be rung and the wording of the recantation will be publicly proclaimed.

ANDREA: I don't believe it.

THE INDIVIDUAL: Because of the crowds collecting in the streets, Signor Galilei will be brought here through the garden door at the back of the palace.

Exit.

ANDREA *suddenly shouting*: The moon is an earth and has no light of its own. Neither has Venus its own light and like the earth it revolves round the sun. And four moons revolve round the planet Jupiter, which is in the region of the fixed stars and is not attached to any crystal sphere. And the sun is the centre of the universe and motionless in its place, and the earth is *not* the centre and is *not* motionless. And he is the one who showed it to us.

THE LITTLE MONK: And force cannot make unseen what has already been seen.

Silence.

FEDERZONI *looks at the sundial in the garden*: Five o'clock.

Virginia prays louder.

ANDREA: I cannot wait any longer. They are killing the truth.

He stops up his ears, as does the little monk. But the bell does not toll. After a pause, filled by Virginia's murmured prayers, Federzoni shakes his head in negation. The others let their hands drop.

FEDERZONI *hoarsely*: Nothing. It is three minutes past five.

ANDREA: He resists.

THE LITTLE MONK: He does not recant.

FEDERZONI: No! Oh, we blessed ones!

They embrace. They are overjoyed.

ANDREA: Well! Force has not prevailed! It cannot do everything! Therefore, stupidity is conquered; it is not invulnerable! Therefore, man is not afraid of death!

FEDERZONI: Now the age of science has really begun. This is the hour of its birth. And think, if he had recanted!

THE LITTLE MONK: I did not say it, but I was filled with fear. I, of so little faith!

ANDREA: But I knew it.

FEDERZONI: It would have been as if night had fallen again just after the sun rose.

ANDREA: As if the mountain had said: I am a sea.

THE LITTLE MONK *kneels down, crying*: Lord, I thank Thee!

ANDREA: But everything has been changed today! Man, tortured man, lifts up his head and says: I can live. So much is gained when only one man stands up and says '*No*'.

At this moment the bell of St. Mark's begins to toll. All stand rigid.

VIRGINIA *stands up*: The bell of Saint Mark's. He is not damned!

From the street outside can be heard the voice of the crier reading Galileo's recantation.

VOICE OF THE CRIER: 'I, Galileo Galilei, teacher of mathematics and physics at the University of Florence, renounce what I have taught, that the sun is the centre of the universe and motionless in its place, and that the earth is not the centre and not motionless. I renounce, abhor and curse, with all my heart and with sincere faith, all these falsehoods and heresies, as well as every other falsehood and every other opinion which is contrary to the teachings of the Holy Church.'

The stage grows dark.
When it grows light again the bell is still tolling, and then stops. Virginia has gone. Galileo's pupils are still there.

FEDERZONI: He never paid you properly for your work. You could neither buy hose nor publish your own work. You suffered because it was 'working for science'.

ANDREA *loudly*: Unhappy the land that has no heroes!

Enter Galileo – completely altered by his trial, almost to the point of being unrecognisable. He has heard Andrea's last sentence. For a moment he pauses at the door for someone to greet him. As no one does, for his pupils shrink back from him, he goes, slowly and unsteadily because of his failing eyesight, to the front where he finds a stool and sits down.

ANDREA: I cannot look at him. He must go.

FEDERZONI: Be calm.

ANDREA *screams at Galileo*: Winebag! Snail-eater! Have you saved your precious skin? *He sits down.* I feel sick.

GALILEO *calmly*: Give him a glass of water.

The little monk goes outside and fetches Andrea a glass of water. The others take no notice of Galileo, who sits listening upon a stool. From far off can be heard the voice of the crier.

ANDREA: I can walk all right, if you help me a bit.

They help him to the door. At this moment Galileo starts to speak.

GALILEO: No. Unhappy the land that is in need of heroes.

Written up in front of the curtain:

Is it not clear that a horse which falls from a height of three or four ells can break its legs, whereas a dog receives no harm; nor does a cat from the height of eight or ten ells, nor a cricket from the top of a tower, nor an ant if it fell from the moon? And just as smaller animals are proportionately stronger and more sturdy than large ones, so too, smaller plants survive better; an oak-tree two hundred ells high could not support branches which were in exact proportion to those of a smaller oak, and Nature could not allow a horse to be as large as twenty horses, nor a giant to be ten times the size of an ordinary man, without changing the proportions of all the members, particularly the bones, which would have to be strengthened out of all proportion to the original enlargement. – The common assumption that large and small machines are equally effective is plainly erroneous.

Galileo, 'Discorsi'.

14

1633–1642. GALILEO GALILEI LIVES IN A COUNTRY
HOUSE NEAR FLORENCE, A PRISONER OF THE INQUISITION
UNTIL HIS DEATH. THE 'DISCORSI'

> Sixteen hundred and thirty-three till
> Sixteen hundred and forty-two
> Galileo Galilei remains a prisoner of the Church
> Up to the day of his death.

A Large Room with Table, Leather Chair and Globe

Galileo, now old and half blind, is experimenting carefully with a little wooden ball on a curved wooden rail. In the ante-room sits a monk on watch. There is a knock at the door. The monk opens it and a peasant enters, carrying two plucked geese. Virginia comes out of the kitchen. She is now about forty.

THE PEASANT: I've been told to deliver these.

VIRGINIA: Who are they from? I haven't ordered any geese.

THE PEASANT: I've been told to say: 'They are from someone passing through.' *Exit.*

Virginia looks at the geese in amazement. The monk takes them from her and examines them suspiciously. Then, reassured, he hands them back to her, and she carries them by their necks to Galileo in the large room.

VIRGINIA: Someone passing through has sent us a present.

GALILEO: What is it?

VIRGINIA: Can't you see?

GALILEO: No. *He walks over.* Geese. Is there a name on them?

VIRGINIA: No.

GALILEO *takes one goose out of her hand*: Heavy. I could eat a bit of that now.

VIRGINIA: You can't be hungry so soon; you've just finished supper. And what's wrong with your eyes again? You ought to have been able to see them from your table.

GALILEO: You are standing in the shadow.

H

VIRGINIA: I am not standing in the shadow.

She carries the geese out.

GALILEO: Cook them with thyme and apples.

VIRGINIA *to the monk*: We must send for the eye-doctor. Father couldn't see the geese from his table.

THE MONK: I shall first have to have the permission of Monsignor Carpula. Has he been writing again himself?

VIRGINIA: No. He has been dictating his book to me; you know that. You have got pages 131 and 132, and they were the last.

THE MONK: He is an old fox.

VIRGINIA: He does nothing against the rules. His repentance is genuine. I watch over him. *She hands him the geese.* Tell them in the kitchen to roast the livers with an apple and an onion. *She goes back to the large room.* And now we'll have a little thought for our eyes and leave that ball alone immediately and dictate a little more of our weekly letter to the archbishop.

GALILEO: I don't really feel well enough. Read me some Horace.

VIRGINIA: Only last week Monsignor Carpula, to whom we owe so much – more vegetables again the other day – said to me that the archbishop asks him every time how you like the questions and quotations he sends you. *She has sat down to take dictation.*

GALILEO: How far had I got?

VIRGINIA: Paragraph four: As regards the attitude of the Holy Church towards the disturbances in the Arsenal at Venice, I am entirely in agreement with the position taken up by Cardinal Spoletti towards the mutinous rope-makers . . .

GALILEO: Yes. *He dictates*: . . . I am entirely in agreement with the position taken up by Cardinal Spoletti towards the mutinous rope-makers, namely, that it is better to dole out soup in the name of Christian brotherly love than to pay them more for their hawsers and bell-ropes. For surely it must be wiser to fortify their faith rather than their greed. The Apostle Paul said: Charity aboundeth. – How does that sound?

VIRGINIA: It's wonderful, father.

GALILEO: You don't think any irony could be read into it?

VIRGINIA: No, the archbishop will be delighted. He is so practical.

GALILEO: I rely on your judgment. What is the next thing?

VIRGINIA: A beautiful saying: 'If I am weak, then I am strong.'

GALILEO: No comment.

VIRGINIA: But why not?

GALILEO: What's the next thing?

VIRGINIA: 'And to know the love of Christ which passeth knowledge.' Epistle to the Ephesians, iii, 19.

GALILEO: I would particularly thank your Eminence for the
wondrous text from the Epistle to the Ephesians. Stimulated
by it, I discovered in our inimitable Imitatio the following.
He quotes from memory: 'He to whom the eternal work speak-
eth, is relieved of much questioning.' May I take this opportunity to speak of myself? I am still being reproached with
having once written a book about the heavenly bodies in the
language of the marketplace. In doing so it was not my intention to suggest or even to approve that books on subjects
so much more important, as for example theology, should be
written in the jargon of pastrycooks. The argument in favour
of the Latin liturgy – namely that because of the universality of
this tongue, the Holy Mass can be heard in the same way by
all peoples – seems to me less happy, since the blasphemers,
who are never at a loss, could object that *no* people can understand the text. I heartily reject cheap lucidity in sacred matters. The Latin of the pulpit, which protects the eternal verities
of the Church against the inquisitiveness of the ignorant,
evokes confidence when spoken by the priestly sons of the
lower classes in the accents of their local dialect. – No, cross
that out.

VIRGINIA: The whole lot?

GALILEO: Everything after 'pastrycooks'.

*There is a knock at the door. Virginia goes into the anteroom. The
monk opens the door. It is Andrea Sarti. He is now a middle-aged
man.*

ANDREA: Good evening. I am about to leave Italy in order to

take up scientific work in Holland, and have been asked to look him up on my way through, so that I can give them news of him.

VIRGINIA: I don't know whether he will see you. You have never come.

ANDREA: Ask him.

Galileo has recognised the voice. He sits motionless. Virginia goes in to him.

GALILEO: Is that Andrea?

VIRGINIA: Yes, shall I send him away?

GALILEO *after a pause*: Bring him in.

Virginia shows Andrea in.

VIRGINIA *to the monk*: He is harmless. He was once his pupil. So now he's his enemy.

GALILEO: Leave him alone with me, Virginia.

VIRGINIA: I want to hear what news he brings. *She sits down.*

ANDREA *coldly*: How are you?

GALILEO: Come closer. What are you doing now? Tell me about your work. I hear it's to do with hydraulics.

ANDREA: Fabricius in Amsterdam has charged me to enquire after your health.

GALILEO: My health is all right. They pay a great deal of attention to me.

ANDREA: I am glad I shall be able to report that you are in good health.

GALILEO: Fabricius will be pleased to hear it. And you can inform him that I live in suitable comfort. By the depth of my repentance I have been able to retain the favour of my superiors so far as to be permitted to engage in scientific work – within certain limits and under the supervision of the Church.

ANDREA: Yes. We, too, have heard that the Church is satisfied with you. Your complete submission has had its effect. It has ensured, as the authorities will have noted with satisfaction, that in Italy no further work containing new ideas has been published since you submitted.

GALILEO *listening*: Unfortunately there are countries which re-

fuse the protection of the Church. I fear that the condemned
teachings may be disseminated there.

ANDREA: There, too, as a result of your recantation, there has been
a set-back most gratifying to the Church.

GALILEO: Really? *Pause.* Nothing of Descartes? Nothing from
Paris?

ANDREA: Yes. At the news of your recantation he stuffed his
treatise on the Nature of Light into a drawer.

A long pause.

GALILEO: I am anxious about certain scientific friends whose feet I
have set upon the path of error. Have they been enlightened
by my recantation?

ANDREA: In order to be able to do scientific work, I intend to go
to Holland. The bull is not permitted to do what Jupiter
does not permit himself.

GALILEO: I understand.

ANDREA: Federzoni is once again grinding lenses in some shop in
Milan.

GALILEO *laughs*: He knows no Latin.

Pause.

ANDREA: Fulganzio, our little monk, has given up research and
has returned to the bosom of the Church.

GALILEO: Yes.

Pause.

GALILEO: My superiors are looking forward to my spiritual re-
cuperation. I am making better progress than might have been
expected.

ANDREA: Ah!

VIRGINIA: The Lord be praised.

GALILEO *harshly*: Go and see to the geese, Virginia.

Virginia goes out angrily. As she passes, the monk speaks to her.

THE MONK: I don't trust that man.

VIRGINIA: He's harmless. You can hear what they say. *As she goes*:
We've got some fresh goat's cheese.

The monk follows her out.

ANDREA: I shall travel through the night in order to be able to cross the frontier tomorrow morning. May I leave?

GALILEO: I don't know why you came, Sarti. In order to upset me? I live cautiously and I think cautiously, ever since I've been here. But in spite of that I have my relapses.

ANDREA: I'd rather not excite you, Signor Galilei.

GALILEO: Barberini called it the itch. He himself was never quite free of it. I've been writing again.

ANDREA: Oh?

GALILEO: I have finished writing the 'Discorsi'.

ANDREA: What? 'The Conversations between two Branches of Science: Mechanics and the Laws of Falling Bodies'? Here?

GALILEO: Oh, they give me paper and quills. My superiors are no fools. They know that ingrained vices cannot be cured overnight. They protect me from unfortunate results by locking it away page by page.

ANDREA: Oh God!

GALILEO: Did you say anything?

ANDREA: They're making you plough water! They give you paper and quills just to soothe you! How could you ever write anything with that prospect before your eyes?

GALILEO: Oh, I am the slave of my habits.

ANDREA: The 'Discorsi' in the hands of the monks! And Amsterdam and London and Prague hungry for them!

GALILEO: I can hear Fabricius wailing, insisting on his pound of flesh, while he sits safely in Amsterdam.

ANDREA: Two new branches of science as good as lost!

GALILEO: It will doubtless cheer him and some others to hear that I risked the last miserable remains of my peace of mind by making a copy, behind my own back so to speak, using up the last ounce of light of the bright nights for the last six months.

ANDREA: You have a copy?

GALILEO: My vanity has hitherto restrained me from destroying it.

ANDREA: Where is it?

GALILEO: 'If thine eye offend thee, pluck it out.' Whoever wrote that knew more about comfort than I. I call it the height of stupidity to hand it over. But since I have never managed to keep myself away from scientific work you might as well have it. The copy is in the globe. If you were to risk taking it to Holland, you would of course have to shoulder full responsibility. In that case you would have bought it from someone who had access to the original in the Holy Office.

Andrea walks across to the globe and takes out the manuscript.

ANDREA: The 'Discorsi'!

He thumbs through the pages.

ANDREA *reads*: 'My project is to establish an entirely new science dealing with a very old subject – Motion. Through experiments I have discovered some of its properties which are worth knowing.'

GALILEO: I had to do something with my time.

ANDREA: This will found a new science of physics.

GALILEO: Stuff it under your coat.

ANDREA: And we thought you had become a renegade! My voice was raised loudest against you!

GALILEO: And quite right, too. I taught you science and I denied the truth.

ANDREA: This changes everything, everything.

GALILEO: Yes?

ANDREA: You concealed the truth. From the enemy. Even in the field of ethics you were a thousand years ahead of us.

GALILEO: Explain that, Andrea.

ANDREA: In common with the man in the street, we said: he will die, but he will never recant. – You came back: I have recanted, but I shall live. – Your hands are tainted, we said. – You say: better tainted than empty.

GALILEO: Better tainted than empty. Sounds realistic. Sounds like me. New science, new ethics.

ANDREA: I of all people ought to have known. I was eleven years old when you sold another man's telescope to the Venetian Senate. And I saw you make immortal use of that instrument.

Your friends shook their heads when you bowed before a child in Florence, but science caught the public fancy. You always laughed at our heroes. 'People that suffer bore me,' you said. 'Misfortune comes from insufficient foresight.' And: 'Taking obstacles into account, the shortest line between two points may be a crooked one.'

GALILEO: I recollect.

ANDREA: Then, in 1633, when it suited you to retract a popular point in your teachings, I should have known that you were only withdrawing from a hopeless political squabble in order to be able to carry on with your real business of science.

GALILEO: Which consists in . . .

ANDREA: . . . The study of the properties of motion, mother of machines, which will make the earth so inhabitable that heaven can be demolished.

GALILEO: Aha.

ANDREA: You thereby gained the leisure to write a scientific work which only you could write. Had you ended in a halo of flames at the stake, the others would have been the victors.

GALILEO: They are the victors. And there is no scientific work which only one man can write.

ANDREA: Then why did you recant?

GALILEO: I recanted because I was afraid of physical pain.

ANDREA: No!

GALILEO: I was shown the instruments.

ANDREA: So there was no plan?

GALILEO: There was none.

Pause.

ANDREA *loudly*: Science knows only one commandment: contribute to science.

GALILEO: And that I have done. Welcome to the gutter, brother in science and cousin in treachery! Do you eat fish? I've got fish. What stinks is not fish but me. I sell cheap; you are a buyer. Oh irresistible sight of a book, the sacred goods! Mouths water, and curses drown. The Great Babylonian, the murderous cow, the scarlet woman, opens her thighs and everything is different! Hallowed be our haggling, white-washing, death-fearing society!

ANDREA: Fear of death is human! Human weaknesses are no concern of science.

GALILEO: No! My dear Sarti, even in my present situation I still feel capable of giving you a few tips about science in general, in which you have involved yourself.

A short pause.

GALILEO *academically, his hands folded over his stomach*: During my free hours, of which I have many, I have gone over my case and have considered how the world of science, in which I no longer count myself, will judge it. Even a wool-merchant, apart from buying cheaply and selling dear, must also be concerned that trade in wool can be carried on unhindered. In this respect the pursuit of science seems to me to require particular courage. It is concerned with knowledge, achieved through doubt. Making knowledge about everything available for everybody, science strives to make sceptics of them all. Now the greater part of the population is kept permanently by their princes, landlords and priests in a nacreous haze of superstition and outmoded words which obscure the machinations of these characters. The misery of the multitude is as old as the hills, and from pulpit and desk is proclaimed as immutable as the hills. Our new device of doubt delighted the great public, which snatched the telescope from our hands and turned it on its tormentors. These selfish and violent men, who greedily exploited the fruits of science to their own use, simultaneously felt the cold eye of science turned on a thousand-year-old, but artificial misery which clearly could be eliminated by eliminating them. They drenched us with their threats and bribes, irresistible to weak souls. But could we deny ourselves to the crowd and still remain scientists? The movements of the stars have become clearer; but to the mass of the people the movements of their masters are still incalculable. The fight over the measurability of the heavens has been won through doubt; but the fight of the Roman housewife for milk is ever and again lost through faith. Science, Sarti, is concerned with both battle-fronts. A humanity which stumbles in this age-old milky mist of superstition and outmoded words, too ignorant to develop fully its own powers, will not be capable of developing the powers of nature which you reveal. What are you working for! I maintain that the only purpose of science is to ease the hardship of human existence. If scientists, intimidated by self-seeking people in power, are content to amass knowledge for the sake of knowledge, then science can become crippled, and your new machines will represent nothing but new means of oppression. With time you may discover all that is to be discovered, and your progress will only be a progression away from mankind. The gulf between you and them can one day become so great that your cry of jubilation over some new achievement may be answered by a universal cry of horror. – I, as a scientist, had a unique opportunity. In my days astronomy reached the marketplaces. In these quite exceptional circumstances, the steadfastness of one man could have shaken the world. If only I had resisted, if only the natural scientists had been able to evolve something like the Hippocratic oath of the doctors, the vow to devote their knowledge wholly to the benefit of mankind! As things now stand, the best one can hope for is for a race of inventive dwarfs who can be hired for anything. Moreover, I am now convinced, Sarti, that I never was in real danger. For a few years I was as strong as the authorities. And I surrendered my knowledge to those in power, to use, or not to use, or to misuse, just as suited their purposes. *Virginia has entered with a dish and stops still.* I have betrayed my profession. A man who does what I have done cannot be tolerated in the ranks of science.

VIRGINIA: You have been received into the ranks of the faithful.

She walks forward and places the dish upon the table.

GALILEO: Right. – I must eat now.

Andrea holds out his hand. Galileo looks at his hand without taking it.

GALILEO: You yourself are a teacher, now. Can you bring yourself to take a hand such as mine? *He walks over to the table.* Someone passing through sent me geese. I still enjoy my food.

ANDREA: So you are no longer of the opinion that a new age has dawned?

GALILEO: I am. Take care when you go through Germany. – Hide the truth under your coat.

ANDREA *incapable of leaving*: With regard to your estimation of the author we were talking about, I don't know how to answer you. But I cannot believe that your murderous analysis will be the last word.

GALILEO: Many thanks, signor. *He begins to eat.*

VIRGINIA *showing Andrea out*: We do not care for visitors from the past. They excite him.

Andrea leaves. Virginia returns.

GALILEO: Have you any idea who could have sent the geese?

VIRGINIA: Not Andrea.

GALILEO: Perhaps not. What is the night like?

VIRGINIA *at the window*: Clear.

15

1637. GALILEO'S BOOK, THE 'DISCORSI', CROSSES THE ITALIAN BORDER

> The great book o'er the border went
> And, good folk, that was the end.
> But we hope you'll keep in mind
> He and I were left behind.
>
> May you now guard Science' light
> Kindle it and use it right
> Lest it be a flame to fall
> Downward to consume us all.

A Small Italian Frontier Town

Early morning. At the frontier turnpike, children are playing. Andrea, a coachman beside him, is waiting for his papers to be examined. He is sitting on a little chest and reading Galileo's manuscript. The travelling-coach stands at the far side of the barrier.

THE CHILDREN *singing*:

> Mary, Mary sat her down
> Had a little old pink gown
> Gown was shabby and bespattered
> But when chilly winter came
> Gown went round her just the same
> Bespattered don't mean tattered.

THE FRONTIER GUARD: Why are you leaving Italy?

ANDREA: I am a scholar.

THE FRONTIER GUARD *to the clerk*: Write under 'reason for journey': scholar. I must search your luggage. *He does so.*

THE FIRST BOY *to Andrea*: You shouldn't sit there. *He points to the hut outside which Andrea is sitting.* A witch lives inside.

THE SECOND BOY: Old Marina is *not* a witch.

THE FIRST BOY: Do you want me to twist your arm?

THE THIRD BOY: She *is* a witch. She flies through the air every night.

THE FIRST BOY: And why can't she get so much as a jug of milk anywhere in town if she isn't a witch?

THE SECOND BOY: How can she fly through the air? No one can do that. *To Andrea*: Can one?

THE FIRST BOY *referring to the second*: That's Giuseppe. He doesn't know a thing because he doesn't go to school because he hasn't a proper pair of breeches.

THE FRONTIER GUARD: What's that book?

ANDREA *without looking up*: It's by the great philosopher Aristotle.

THE FRONTIER GUARD *suspiciously*: What sort of a fellow's he?

ANDREA: He's dead.

The boys, to mock Andrea as he reads, prance round pretending to read books at the same time.

THE FRONTIER GUARD *to the clerk*: See whether there's anything about religion in it.

THE CLERK *leafing through it*: I can find nothing.

THE FRONTIER GUARD: There's little enough point in all this searching! Nobody's going to show us openly things that he wants to hide. *To Andrea.* You must sign that we've searched everything.

Andrea stands up hesitantly and goes, still reading, into the house with the frontier guard.

THE THIRD BOY *to the clerk, pointing at the chest*: Look, there's something else, look!

THE CLERK: Wasn't that there before?

THE THIRD BOY: The Devil put it there. It's a chest.

THE SECOND BOY: No, it belongs to the stranger.

THE THIRD BOY: I wouldn't go in there. She's bewitched the coachman's old nags. I looked through that hole in the roof which the snowstorm made and heard them coughing.

THE CLERK *who has almost reached the chest, hesitates and turns back*: Devil's work, eh? Well, we can't examine everything. Or where would we be?

Andrea returns with a jug of milk. He sits down again on the chest and continues to read.

THE FRONTIER GUARD *following him with papers*: Close up the boxes again. Have we everything?

THE CLERK: Everything.

THE SECOND BOY *to Andrea*: You're a scholar. You tell us – can one fly through the air?

ANDREA: Wait a moment.

THE FRONTIER GUARD: You can pass.

The luggage is collected by the coachman. Andrea picks up the chest and is about to go.

THE FRONTIER GUARD: Stop! What's that chest?

ANDREA *resuming his book*: It's books.

THE FIRST BOY: It's bewitched.

THE FRONTIER GUARD: Nonsense. How could she bewitch a chest?

THE THIRD BOY: She can if the Devil helps her!

THE FRONTIER GUARD *laughs*: That won't work here. *To the clerk*: Open it up. *The chest is opened.*

THE FRONTIER GUARD *morosely*: How many are there?

ANDREA: Thirty-four.

THE FRONTIER GUARD *to the clerk*: How long will you take over them?

THE CLERK *who has begun to rummage superficially in the chest*: All printed already. You can certainly say goodbye to your breakfast; when am I going to have time to get over to the coachman and collect these arrears of toll money from the selling up of his house if I have to wade through all these books?

THE FRONTIER GUARD: Yes, we must have the money. *He pushes the books with his foot.* Well, what a lot of stuff there must be in them! *To the coachman*: Get on!

Andrea, carrying the chest, goes with the coachman across the frontier. On the other side he puts Galileo's manuscript in his travelling bag.

THE THIRD BOY *points at the jug which Andrea has left behind*: Look!

THE FIRST BOY: And the chest has gone! You see, it *was* the Devil.

ANDREA *turning round*: No, it was me. You must learn to open your eyes. The milk is paid for and so is the jug. The old woman can have it. Yes, and I haven't yet answered your question, Giuseppe. One cannot fly through the air on a broomstick. It must at least have a machine on it. And as yet there is no such machine. Perhaps there never will be, for man is too heavy. But, of course, one cannot tell. We don't know nearly enough, Giuseppe. We are really only at the beginning.

Methuen's Modern Plays

EDITED BY JOHN CULLEN AND GEOFFREY STRACHAN